INDIAN JEWELRY MAKING

VOLUME I

by
OSCAR T. BRANSON

**INDIAN JEWELRY MAKING
VOLUME I**

Copyright ©1977
by
Oscar T. Branson

All rights reserved throughout the world
under
International and Pan American Conventions.

ISBN 0-918080-15-0 (softcover edition)

First Printing 25,000 copies
Second Printing 10,000 copies
Third Printing 10,000 copies
Fourth Printing 5,000 copies

Photography
by
NAURICE KOONCE
Tucson, Arizona

Other books by Oscar T. Branson

TURQUOISE, THE GEM of the CENTURIES
ISBN 0-918080-01-0 (softcover edition)

FETISHES and CARVINGS of the SOUTHWEST
ISBN 0-918080-04-5 (softcover edition)

INDIAN JEWELRY MAKING   VOLUME II
ISBN 0-918080-15-0 (softcover edition)

WHAT YOU NEED TO KNOW ABOUT YOUR GOLD AND SILVER
ISBN 0-918080-44-4 (softcover edition)

TREASURE CHEST PUBLICATIONS, INC.

P.O. Box 5250 — Tucson, Arizona 85703

Printed by Walsworth Publishing Co., Marceline, Missouri

INTRODUCTION

Southwestern Indian jewelry has probably become the foremost American craft. It has not only become a monetary investment for millions of Americans but an investment in beauty they can enjoy every minute of the day. We think of it as truly American, and it really is. The squash blossom necklace is composed of three main components all of foreign origins. They are put together in a very unique and original manner. Possibly nowhere else in the world has such a beautiful piece of jewelry been evolved which uniquely belongs to a single people, the Navajo Indians.

The concha belt is another example of the foreign elements of design which the Navajo adopted, changed and developed into a very unique piece of jewelry and a symbol of the Navajo nation. True, there are silver belts made and worn by tribes and people around the world but none so unique or individual and even wearable by almost anyone as is the Navajo concha belt. The bracelets that have been designed and made by the Indians, especially the Navajo but also all the Indians of the Southwest, are again unique creations, indigenous to the Southwest even if some of the original ideas are borrowed. They combine the elements of beautiful white silver and lovely blue turquoise, which to them symbolizes the beautiful Western skies. Nowhere in the world is the sky more deep turquoise blue and the clouds more pure silver white than over the Southwest Indian country. It is no wonder living among this natural beauty that such uniquely beautiful jewelry be developed, made and worn by every Indian man, woman, and child and usually in great profusion. Traditional styles and designs were mostly used in the illustrations of this book. There has been no drastic change in Indian jewelry design during the last fifty years although styles are constantly changing under social and economic pressures. There has been a trend by some silversmiths to add numerous elements such as leaves, feathers, flowers, but this has not really altered the design; only a cluttering has happened of what could have been good design. At the present time there are many young and brilliant Indian jewelers. Their creations foretell great and surprising changes in the future design of Indian jewelry. But even with the prospect of great change in the future, the traditional designs and ideas will always be the foundation to the inspiration and will increasingly be used and collected. This book is intended as a step-by-step how-to-do-it method of making jewlery. Not only Indian jewelry but any kind of jewelry. Where only one method or technique has been illustrated, there could be several different ways to do the same thing. The most important thing this book is intended to provide is the basic knowledge of how jewelry is made so one can judge if it is well made and of basically good design.

The rings pictured around the border are an attempt to illustrate the chronology of ring making by the Navajo Indians of the Southwest. The dates are at best only approximate as the styles and history of development varied greatly during the same period in time according to the areas across the vast Navajo reservation.

NAVAJO SILVERSMITH WORKSHOP OF 1870 TO 1920
THE BELLOWS AND CHARCOAL SOLDERING PERIOD

At this time the only known method for soldering jewelry was to heat the object over burning charcoal and intensifying the heat with air from the hand bellows. This was the period when tools and silver were scarce. Many of the tools were hand made from pieces of scrap iron recovered from old wagon or harness fittings. Files were almost a luxury. The only source of silver was Mexican or American coins and the solder was home made by melting together coins and about 20% cartridge brass.

Even with these crude tools and usually under difficult circumstances the Navajo made some of their most beautiful jewelry.

All the soldering was done by using the bellows and charcoal.

SILVERWORK OF THE NAVAJO SILVERSMITH OF THE 1870-1920 PERIOD

Silver horsebridle or headstall

At this time very little turquoise was available and consequently very little was set because most had to be cut and polished with crude tools. Juan Lorenzo Hubbell of Ganado, Arizona, sent Cerrillos turquoise to Germany to have it cut and polished, then returned and it was given out to silversmiths to mount in jewelry. He also imported turquoise from Persia.

Whisker pullers or tweezers

Powder and shot measure for old muzzle loading guns

Silver snuff or "tobacco" canteen

Moccasin buttons

Manta or scarf pin

Old style loop ear rings

Background is a late classic Navajo child's wearing blanket of homespun made about 1880. Courtesy Selser Gallery, Tucson, Arizona.

NAVAJO INDIAN JEWELRY OF THE 1920 TO 1940 PERIOD

The unlimited artistic abilities of the Navajo silversmith were given full amplitude with the availability of finer tools and materials.

Cut and polished turquoise was relatively inexpensive and stones of all sizes, shapes and colors were used in an almost experimental but very artistic fashion.

Every silversmith had unlimited numbers of stamps and dies because he usually made his own. The concha belt became the show piece of design and with it the art of die stamping attained its peak during this period.

A silver table bell of about 1925

The background is a Navajo Indian rug woven near the Ganado Trading Post in Arizona in about 1925. The deep red color was introduced by Juan Lorenzo Hubbell and is popularly known as Ganado Red.

The demand for the tourist trade made a great impact on the design and quality of jewelry turned out and jewelry classes at the Albuquerque and Santa Fe Indian Schools produced many notable silversmiths.

THE NAVAJO SILVERSMITH WORKSHOP OF 1940 TO 1976

THE PREST-O-LITE OR ACETYLENE TORCH PERIOD

This is the period when the gasoline blowtorch was replaced by the safer, hotter and more precise flame of the acetylene torch.

Set of ring gauges

Since Juan Lorenzo Hubbell furnished cut turquoise to the Navajo silversmith, almost all the stones were cut in shops off the reservation and not by the Indian who made the piece of jewelry. The Zuni Indians however cut all their turquoise stones. Until 1950 almost all the turquoise stones used were symmetrically cut. As demand increased the turquoise was cut mostly to get the greatest weight in a so called "free form" cut and unfortunately many times by cutters who had never set a stone and knew nothing of the technical aspects of jewelry making.

Striker or lighter

The acetylene or Prest-O-Lite soldering torch became available at this time and made silver working much easier, but a skilled craftsman could do all the soldering techniques with a gasoline blowtorch that he could do with an acetylene torch. Better tools, pliers, scissors, fluxes, mandrels, hammers, anvils, and saw blades made the work easier and quicker.

The most important improvement other than the acetylene torch was the availability of sheet silver in almost any thickness and silver wire of every gauge.

Silversmiths combo bench pin, ring and bracelet mandrel.
Courtesy Coffey's Lapidary, Spring Valley, California.

Prest-O-Lite or acetylene tank and torch

Jewelers work bench.
Courtesy Starr Gem Inc.
Tucson, Arizona.

EMBOSSED BUTTONS

All the buttons on this page were made by the use of male and female embossing dies.

Four different sizes of buttons can be made with this male punch and female die with cavities sunk to four different depths.

Most small buttons can be made from pieces of scrap silver from other jewelry operations.

Round disks must be used in this die set to make buttons.

These buttons were all made from Mexican or American coins. Many hundreds of thousands of silver dimes and quarters and some fifty cent pieces were and still are worn by the Navajos by simply soldering a copper ring to the back. This is not against the law as some people mistakenly believe.

This is a simple doming punch and die.

The first buttons worn by the Navajos were of this type. They were probably domed in a wooden block.

These are strings of old buttons taken in pawn and not redeemed.

Male and female stamping dies courtesy of Tucker Tool Company, Prescott, Arizona.

KACHINA MASK BUTTON

The designs for these buttons are taken from the Kachina masks of the Hopi and Zuni Indians. A few were made at Hopi during the 1930's.

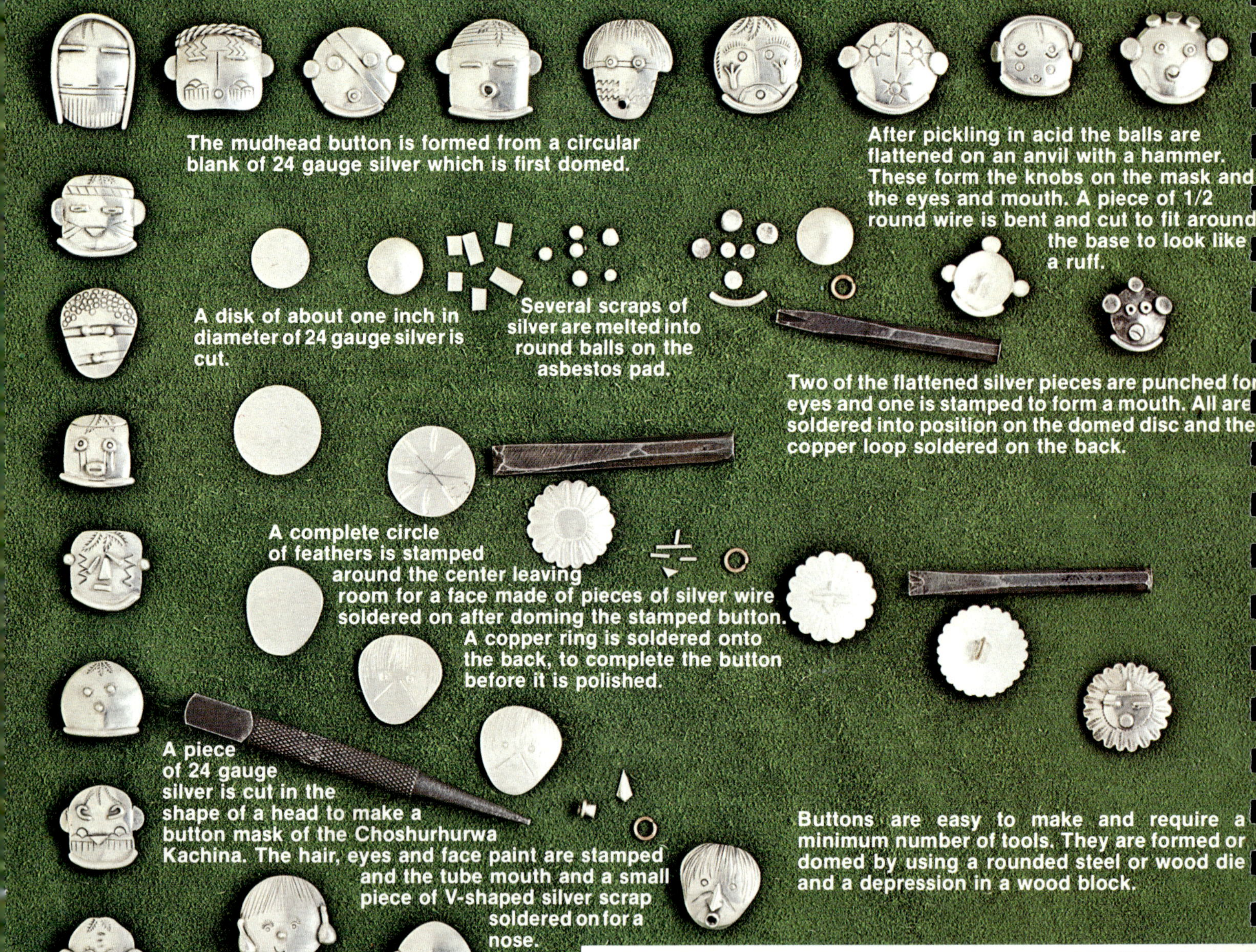

The mudhead button is formed from a circular blank of 24 gauge silver which is first domed.

After pickling in acid the balls are flattened on an anvil with a hammer. These form the knobs on the mask and the eyes and mouth. A piece of 1/2 round wire is bent and cut to fit around the base to look like a ruff.

A disk of about one inch in diameter of 24 gauge silver is cut.

Several scraps of silver are melted into round balls on the asbestos pad.

Two of the flattened silver pieces are punched for eyes and one is stamped to form a mouth. All are soldered into position on the domed disc and the copper loop soldered on the back.

A complete circle of feathers is stamped around the center leaving room for a face made of pieces of silver wire soldered on after doming the stamped button. A copper ring is soldered onto the back, to complete the button before it is polished.

A piece of 24 gauge silver is cut in the shape of a head to make a button mask of the Choshurhurwa Kachina. The hair, eyes and face paint are stamped and the tube mouth and a small piece of V-shaped silver scrap soldered on for a nose.

Buttons are easy to make and require a minimum number of tools. They are formed or domed by using a rounded steel or wood die and a depression in a wood block.

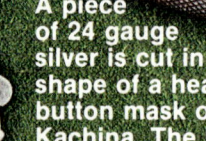

KAIBAB MOCCASINS

The designs need not be limited to Kachina masks. Caricatures of one's self or friends can easily be made.

Tawa Kachina mask moccasin buttons.

Moccasins and buttons courtesy of the Kaibab Shop, Tucson, Arizona.

12

DIE STAMPED BUTTONS THAT ARE DOMED OR PUNCHED AFTER STAMPING

All the buttons on this page were stamped with a rosette stamp on a flat surface or anvil and later shaped, domed or cone punched.

Diamond center punch.

The rosette is outlined by stamping with a small die. The button is trimmed with tin snips or jewelers saw and filed, outlining the design.

It is then domed in a wooden block with a smooth round punch. A copper ring is soldered to the back of the button and it is then buffed and polished.

A rectangular piece of silver sheet of 24 or 22 gauge is centered and stamped with the rosette stamp on a flat anvil.

This particular die has an embossed diamond center which is punched by fitting the stamped piece back onto the die and embossing it with the special diamond tool.

These buttons were made from pieces of silver punched by a smooth surface cone punch into a female rosette die. This type of button has been very popular among the Navajo and many thousands have been made and worn.

These three flat face dies are designed to stamp rosettes in silver on a flat anvil. Afterwards the rosettes are domed.

This is a string of miniature buttons probably made for a doll or a little girl's wrists.

These are old buttons made like the rest of the buttons pictured on this page. They were pawned years ago. Each string represents the decoration removed from a velvet blouse and pawned at the trading post and never redeemed. This happens when the owner needs money or when a blouse and buttons become old and worn and the owner simply wants a new blouse with new buttons.

These are very old buttons taken from a decayed piece of leather found in the Ute country of southwest Colorado. They were made by engraving the outline of a star and then domed and a copper leather tack was lead soldered onto the back.

Male and female stamping dies courtesy of Tucker Tool Company, Prescott, Arizona.

CHAIN MAKING

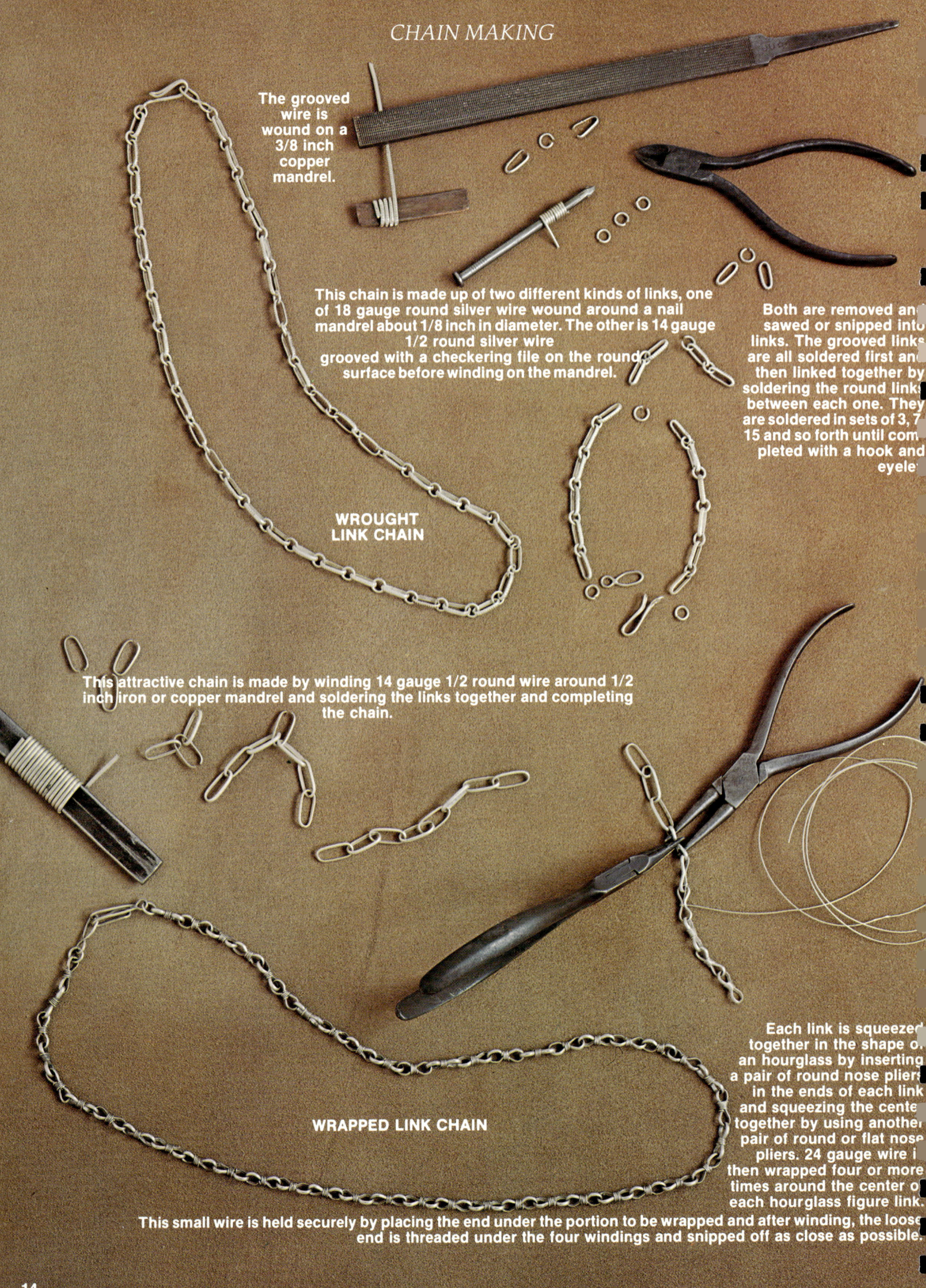

The grooved wire is wound on a 3/8 inch copper mandrel.

This chain is made up of two different kinds of links, one of 18 gauge round silver wire wound around a nail mandrel about 1/8 inch in diameter. The other is 14 gauge 1/2 round silver wire grooved with a checkering file on the round surface before winding on the mandrel.

Both are removed and sawed or snipped into links. The grooved links are all soldered first and then linked together by soldering the round links between each one. They are soldered in sets of 3, 7, 15 and so forth until completed with a hook and eyelet.

WROUGHT LINK CHAIN

This attractive chain is made by winding 14 gauge 1/2 round wire around 1/2 inch iron or copper mandrel and soldering the links together and completing the chain.

WRAPPED LINK CHAIN

Each link is squeezed together in the shape of an hourglass by inserting a pair of round nose pliers in the ends of each link and squeezing the center together by using another pair of round or flat nose pliers. 24 gauge wire is then wrapped four or more times around the center of each hourglass figure link. This small wire is held securely by placing the end under the portion to be wrapped and after winding, the loose end is threaded under the four windings and snipped off as close as possible.

CHAIN MAKING

THE LONG LINK ROUND WIRE CHAIN

Usually sterling silver wire of 18 or 20 gauge is used if you wish to make a heavy substantial chain. Use finer wire if you like a lighter chain.

...convenient mandrel to wind and shape the chain ...can be made from short lengths of flattened ...pper tubing. It comes in several sizes, 1/4 inch ...ube is used here to make a link about 1/2 ...nch long. The wire, after being wound ...n the copper, can be slightly ...attened with a mallet to ...xpand it so it will slide ...ff easily.

A number of links are soldered singly and two soldered links joined for a threesome.

Two threes are joined to make seven.

Two sevens are joined to make fifteen and only four or five of these are needed to make a chain of sufficient length for a pendant or naja.

Each coil is snipped to form a link or the entire wrapping is put in a vise and cut into links with a slitting saw.

The hooks and eyes are formed from the same gauge wire using a pair of round nose pliers, shaping, soldering and bending as shown.

...ound links can ...easily made by ...nding the wire ...a convenient size ...l, cutting with a ...all slitting or jewelers ...w or hammering slightly ...h a rawhide mallet and ...pping the round wire from ...e nail and snipping each link.

These can be put together as a round link chain or with oval links or in many different combinations.

THE ROUND AND OVAL LINK CHAIN

Links can be made of wire of any shape or size, twisted, flat, hammered 1/2 round, half round, square or any shape that suits the imagination.

All chains should be pickled in acid after soldering. A fairly good polish can be given to chains by drawing them a number of times thru a rouge-saturated polishing cloth. WARNING! Never attempt to polish a chain on a cloth buffing wheel unless it is wrapped securely around a board and the ends held tightly with both hands.

Chain making is one of the simplest and easiest of all the arts of the silversmith but probably the most tedious.

CHAIN MAKING

ONE HALF ROUND WIRE LONG LINK CHAIN

All wire used to make the chains is of sterling silver.

This chain is made from 12 gauge 1/2 round silver wire, wound around a 1/2 inch copper mandrel.

The formed wire is slipped from the mandrel and each link snipped or sawed at the end.

A number of links are soldered and then two links are joined by a third link.

These sections of three links each are joined until the chain is of proper length.

This chain is made by winding 18 gauge round wire around a 7/8 inch mandrel made from a piece of flattened copper tubing.

THE MONEY CHAIN

Each link is soldered separately.

To finish, a hook is soldered on one end and an eyelet on the other.

Each link is bent into a figure eight by the use of round nose pliers. Then each figure eight is bent in the middle to form a double loop.

The origin of this chain goes back many hundreds of years. This design, known throughout the Middle East, was popular with the Moors and later with the early Spanish. It was made in both silver and gold and was known as the money chain as it is fairly easy to remove a link or a number of links and use in place of money.

This is the type of chain that was used on Spanish and Mexican jackets and trousers to fasten the popular pomegranate button which later became the Navajo squash blossom.

Each link is hooked into the loop of another link without soldering so that any number of links could be easily added or removed.

Easy removal of links is prevented by soldering at both ends round links with hook and eye.

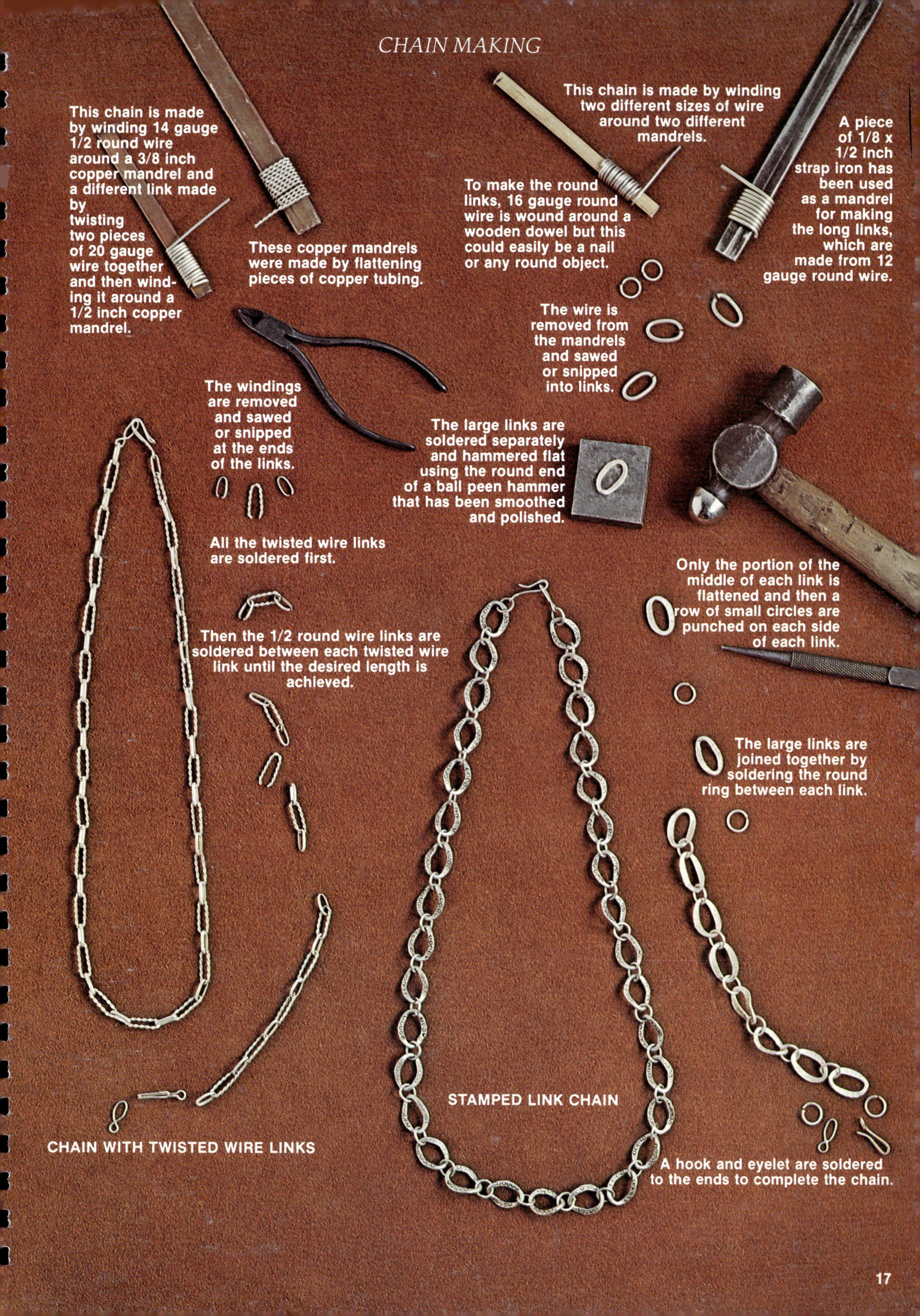

CHAIN MAKING

This chain is made by winding 14 gauge 1/2 round wire around a 3/8 inch copper mandrel and a different link made by twisting two pieces of 20 gauge wire together and then winding it around a 1/2 inch copper mandrel.

These copper mandrels were made by flattening pieces of copper tubing.

This chain is made by winding two different sizes of wire around two different mandrels.

To make the round links, 16 gauge round wire is wound around a wooden dowel but this could easily be a nail or any round object.

A piece of 1/8 x 1/2 inch strap iron has been used as a mandrel for making the long links, which are made from 12 gauge round wire.

The wire is removed from the mandrels and sawed or snipped into links.

The windings are removed and sawed or snipped at the ends of the links.

The large links are soldered separately and hammered flat using the round end of a ball peen hammer that has been smoothed and polished.

All the twisted wire links are soldered first.

Only the portion of the middle of each link is flattened and then a row of small circles are punched on each side of each link.

Then the 1/2 round wire links are soldered between each twisted wire link until the desired length is achieved.

The large links are joined together by soldering the round ring between each link.

CHAIN WITH TWISTED WIRE LINKS

STAMPED LINK CHAIN

A hook and eyelet are soldered to the ends to complete the chain.

17

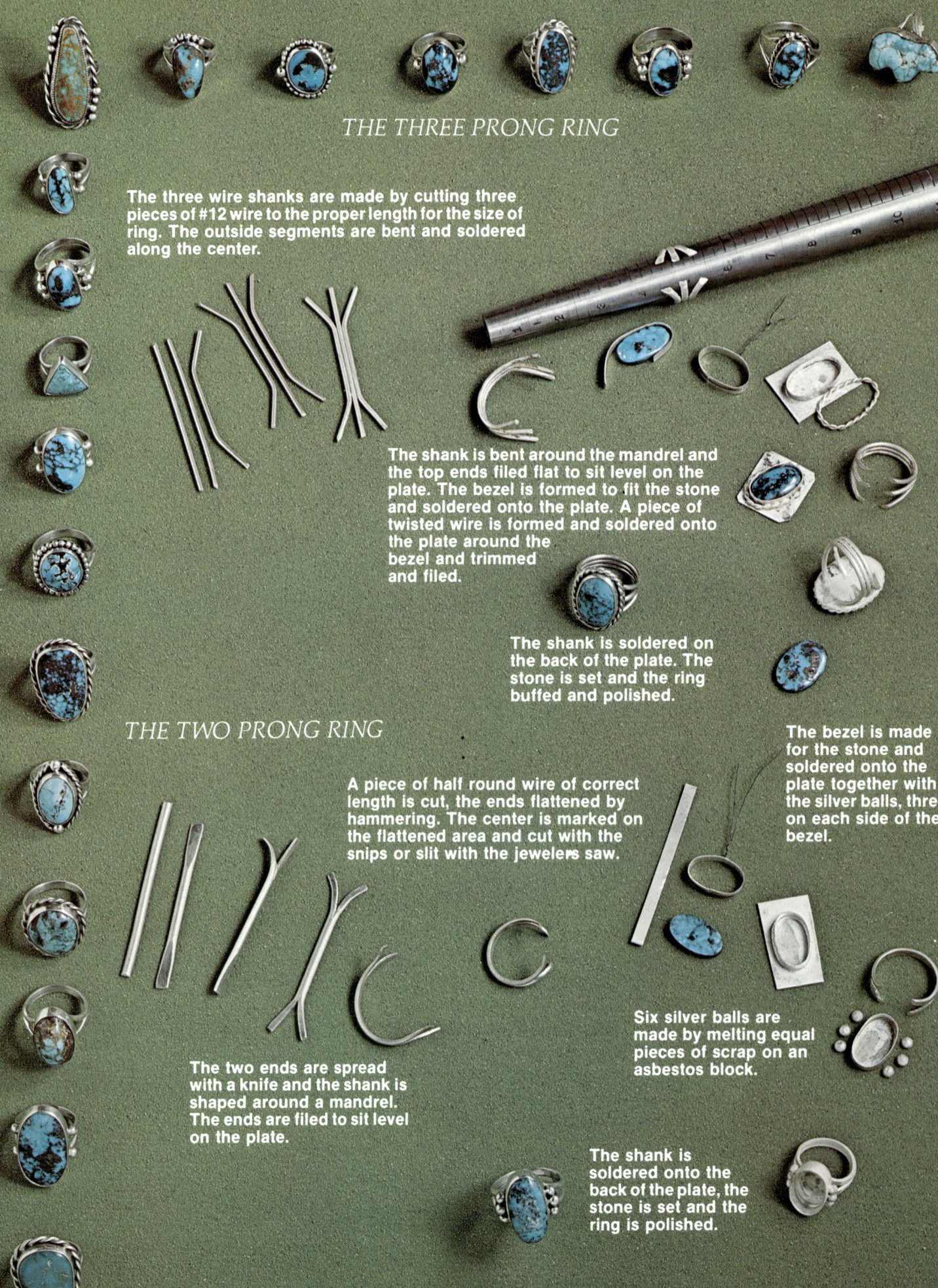

THE THREE PRONG RING

The three wire shanks are made by cutting three pieces of #12 wire to the proper length for the size of ring. The outside segments are bent and soldered along the center.

The shank is bent around the mandrel and the top ends filed flat to sit level on the plate. The bezel is formed to fit the stone and soldered onto the plate. A piece of twisted wire is formed and soldered onto the plate around the bezel and trimmed and filed.

The shank is soldered on the back of the plate. The stone is set and the ring buffed and polished.

The bezel is made for the stone and soldered onto the plate together with the silver balls, three on each side of the bezel.

THE TWO PRONG RING

A piece of half round wire of correct length is cut, the ends flattened by hammering. The center is marked on the flattened area and cut with the snips or slit with the jewelers saw.

Six silver balls are made by melting equal pieces of scrap on an asbestos block.

The two ends are spread with a knife and the shank is shaped around a mandrel. The ends are filed to sit level on the plate.

The shank is soldered onto the back of the plate, the stone is set and the ring is polished.

SINGLE STONE BAND RING

A pattern is made from stiff paper and marked on 18g. silver sheet.

The ring blank is cut out with a jewelers saw and a design stamped on the shank.

The ring can be initially bent by using this convenient hardwood bending jig. The final round shaping can be done on a ring mandrel.

The stone selected, a bezel is made, soldered and filed to fit the curvature of the top of the ring.

The bezel is soldered onto the top of the shank with the twisted wire decoration around it.

The stone is set and the ring is polished.

BUTTON TOP BAND RING

Other designs are stamped onto the shank and it is hammered around a ring mandrel. The shank ends soldered together and to complete, round the ring on the mandrel, buff, and then polish.

One of the simplest and most popular rings to make is designed around a button die.

A ring blank is cut from 18g. sheet silver and the ring centered and stamped into a small button die.

The ring is bent on the mandrel and soldered.

The ring shank is filed smooth and polished.

19

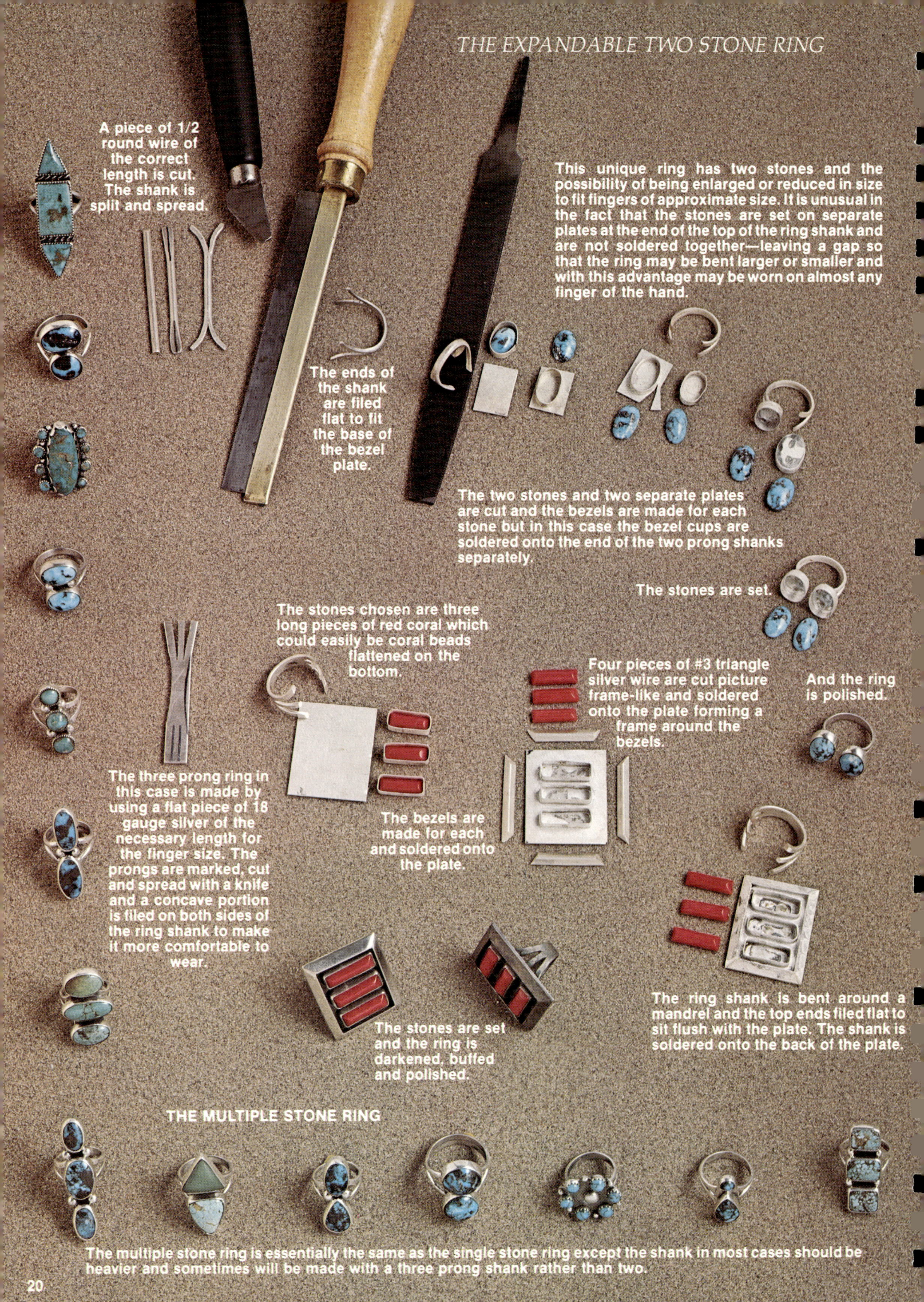

THE EXPANDABLE TWO STONE RING

A piece of 1/2 round wire of the correct length is cut. The shank is split and spread.

This unique ring has two stones and the possibility of being enlarged or reduced in size to fit fingers of approximate size. It is unusual in the fact that the stones are set on separate plates at the end of the top of the ring shank and are not soldered together—leaving a gap so that the ring may be bent larger or smaller and with this advantage may be worn on almost any finger of the hand.

The ends of the shank are filed flat to fit the base of the bezel plate.

The two stones and two separate plates are cut and the bezels are made for each stone but in this case the bezel cups are soldered onto the end of the two prong shanks separately.

The stones are set.

The stones chosen are three long pieces of red coral which could easily be coral beads flattened on the bottom.

Four pieces of #3 triangle silver wire are cut picture frame-like and soldered onto the plate forming a frame around the bezels.

And the ring is polished.

The three prong ring in this case is made by using a flat piece of 18 gauge silver of the necessary length for the finger size. The prongs are marked, cut and spread with a knife and a concave portion is filed on both sides of the ring shank to make it more comfortable to wear.

The bezels are made for each and soldered onto the plate.

The stones are set and the ring is darkened, buffed and polished.

The ring shank is bent around a mandrel and the top ends filed flat to sit flush with the plate. The shank is soldered onto the back of the plate.

THE MULTIPLE STONE RING

The multiple stone ring is essentially the same as the single stone ring except the shank in most cases should be heavier and sometimes will be made with a three prong shank rather than two.

THE MAN'S RING

This is a broken paring knife which is a very useful tool to the silversmith. In this case it is used to spread the shank segments when the shank is being held in a vise.

The mans style ring is usually larger and heavier than other types of rings and quite frequently the stones are rectangular or square.

Two triangular pieces of 20 gauge silver are cut to fit over the spread shank.

A die of proper triangular design is stamped into each of the triangular pieces which are then soldered onto the shank and filed to fit.

A piece of 16 gauge silver of the correct length is cut about 1/4 inch wide. It is marked, sawed and spread with a broken knife.

The plate is trimmed and soldered onto the shank.

The shank is then formed around a mandrel and filed flat to fit the plate.

The stone is set and the ring polished.

A stone is chosen, a bezel is made and soldered onto a plate with two pieces of decoration for each side. In this case it is two short pieces of stamped triangle wire.

A rawhide mallet is used to form the silver band around a ring mandrel.

The strip is bent around a ring mandrel and soldered.

The ring should be hammered to perfect roundness after soldering.

A piece of 16 gauge silver cut 1/2 inch wide and long enough to fit around the finger.

The design is stamped onto the strip while flat.

The design is darkened and the ring buffed and polished.

THE SILVER BAND RING

THE DIE STAMPED BRACELET

This bracelet was the type first made by the Navajo Indians of the Southwest.

It is one of the simplest bracelets to make and requires only a few tools to complete. It is attractive and can be worn equally well by both men and women, and is often worn in pairs. It was probably the first type to be set with turquoise and can be set with one or even dozens of stones.

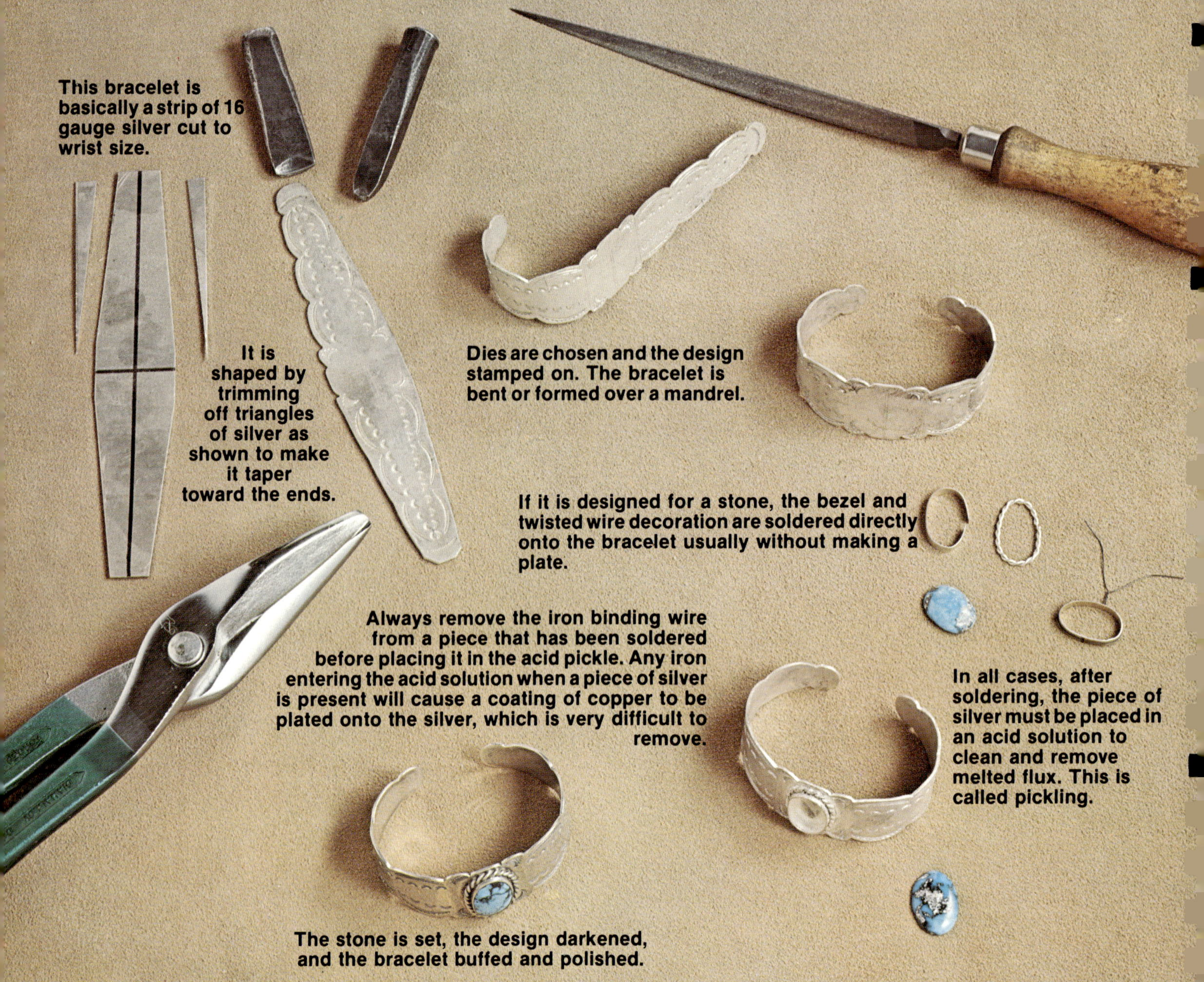

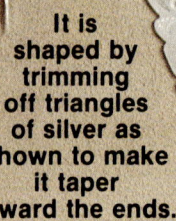

This bracelet is basically a strip of 16 gauge silver cut to wrist size.

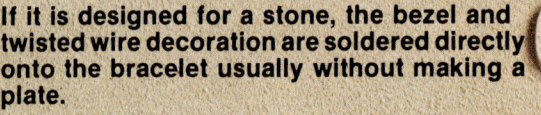

It is shaped by trimming off triangles of silver as shown to make it taper toward the ends.

Dies are chosen and the design stamped on. The bracelet is bent or formed over a mandrel.

If it is designed for a stone, the bezel and twisted wire decoration are soldered directly onto the bracelet usually without making a plate.

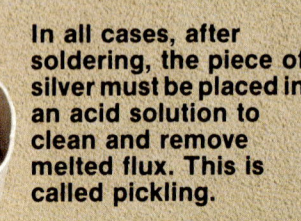

Always remove the iron binding wire from a piece that has been soldered before placing it in the acid pickle. Any iron entering the acid solution when a piece of silver is present will cause a coating of copper to be plated onto the silver, which is very difficult to remove.

In all cases, after soldering, the piece of silver must be placed in an acid solution to clean and remove melted flux. This is called pickling.

The stone is set, the design darkened, and the bracelet buffed and polished.

This bracelet was purchased from a Navajo Indian in Antonito, Colorado in 1929.

BRACELET MAKING

The multiple stone bracelet based on the decorated or stamped triangle wire shank is one of the most attractive and graceful bracelets made by the Southwestern Indians.

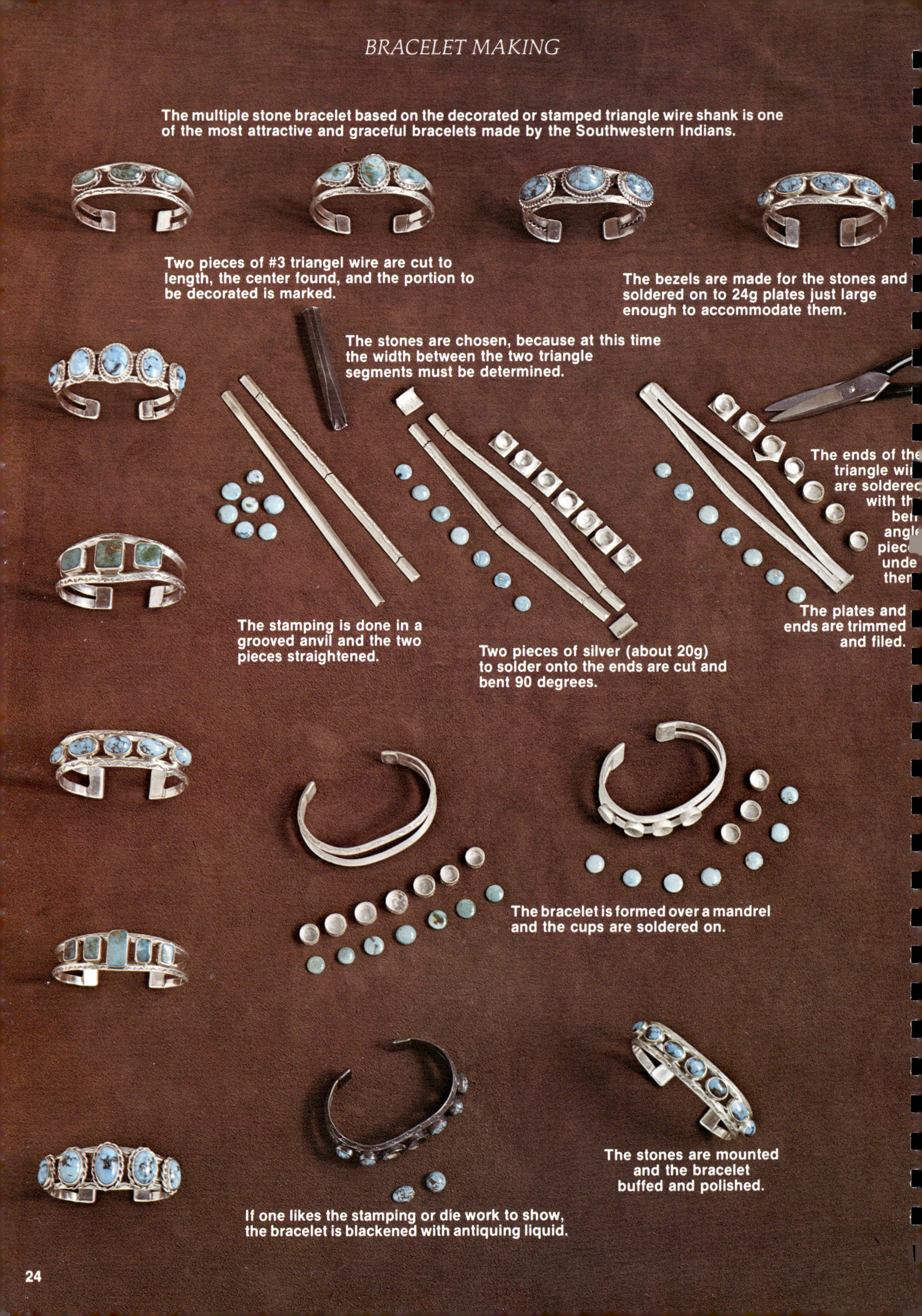

Two pieces of #3 triangel wire are cut to length, the center found, and the portion to be decorated is marked.

The bezels are made for the stones and soldered on to 24g plates just large enough to accommodate them.

The stones are chosen, because at this time the width between the two triangle segments must be determined.

The ends of the triangle wire are soldered with the bent angle piece under them.

The stamping is done in a grooved anvil and the two pieces straightened.

Two pieces of silver (about 20g) to solder onto the ends are cut and bent 90 degrees.

The plates and ends are trimmed and filed.

The bracelet is formed over a mandrel and the cups are soldered on.

The stones are mounted and the bracelet buffed and polished.

If one likes the stamping or die work to show, the bracelet is blackened with antiquing liquid.

THE CAST SILVER BRACELET WITH STONES

These cast silver bracelet shanks were made by Navajo Indians melting scrap silver from other jewelry-making operations and pouring it into hand carved tufa molds.

Many traders buy them and have other Indian silversmiths add large stones or a number of stones.

They are usually heavier in weight and have a massive character that other bracelets do not have.

A very attractive bracelet is made by soldering together a number, in this case eight, 1/2 round silver wire segments about 5¾ inches long.

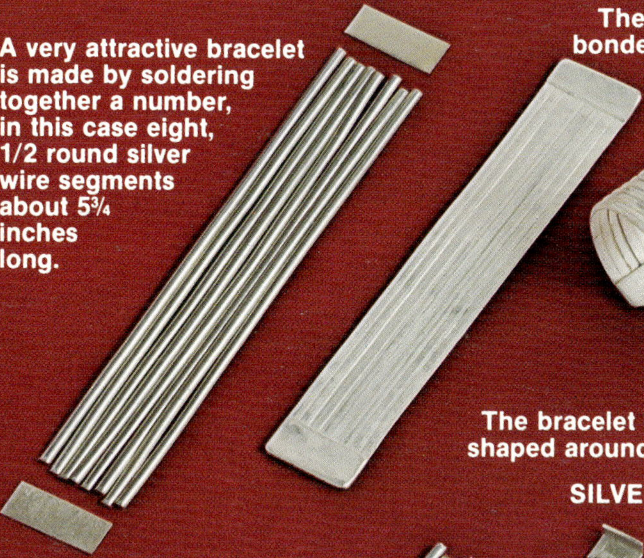

The ends are additionally bonded together by soldering flat silver strips along the ends.

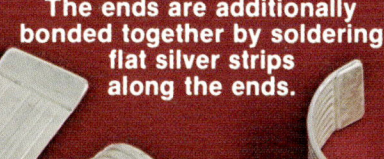  

The bracelet is pickled, filed and shaped around a bracelet mandrel.

If desired, a stone can be added by soldering onto the bracelet a plate with a bezel made to fit the stone.

SILVER WIRE BRACELETS

The round wire bracelet is made by cutting two lengths of 8 gauge round silver wire and a length of twisted wire which should be about the same diameter of the solid wire.

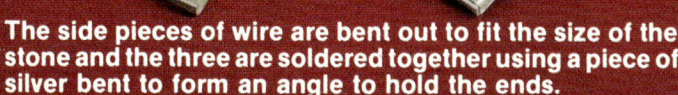  

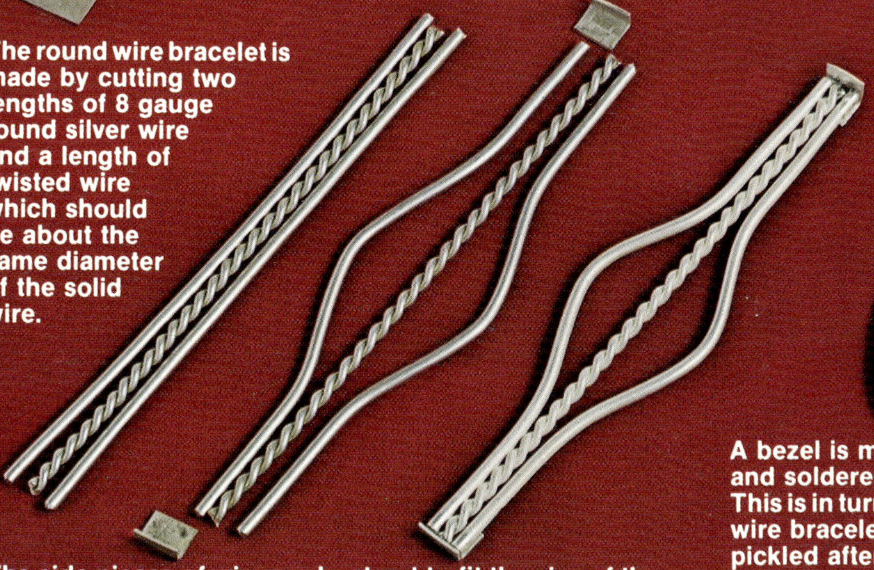

A bezel is made for the stone and soldered onto the plate. This is in turn soldered onto the wire bracelet shank, and pickled after each soldering operation.

The stone is set and the bracelet buffed and polished.

The side pieces of wire are bent out to fit the size of the stone and the three are soldered together using a piece of silver bent to form an angle to hold the ends.

These four bracelets are only a few of the many possible designs using the wire bracelet shank.

25

THE NAVAJO CONCHA

This is the circular or ovate silver metal plate that gives the belt its name. The Spanish word "concha" means shell.

An oval outline is drawn around the rosette by measuring equally from the ends of each segment.

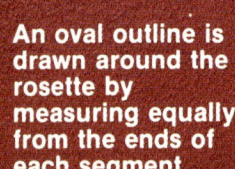

A piece of 18 gauge silver sheet is cut to 2¼ x 2½ inches. The center is marked and the rosette is stamped in the center of the rectangular piece of silver by using a male and female punch and die and a very heavy hammer.

Several dies are selected for the appropriate design and stamped into the silver as shown.

The oval is cut along the outline by using either a jewelers saw or a pair of tin snips.

Scallops are filed around the edge of the concha outlining the stamped design.

It takes 8 conchas and 9 spacers or butterflies and a buckle of this size to make a 30-inch belt.

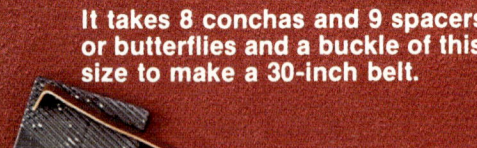

Stones are selected, bezels made and soldered onto plates which are trimmed and soldered onto the center of the rosette.

A copper belt loop or hasp is made by cutting 18 gauge copper sheet in strips ¼ inch wide and forming around a piece of old 1-inch file. The hasps are soldered onto the back of the conchas perpendicular to the long axis.

The conchas pictured here are only a few of the many hundreds of designs possible. Almost every concha belt seen displays a different design confirming the imaginative ingenuity of the Indian mind.

Each stone is set into the bezel and the concha buffed and polished.

Stamps and Dies, courtesy of Tucker Tool Co., Prescott, Arizona.

THE NAVAJO CONCHA BELT BUCKLE

A piece of 18 gauge silver sheet is cut 2 inches by 2¾. The center is marked and the belt opening marked 1 inch by 1¾ inches.

2 sets of bicurvate dies are selected to make the main design.

Female bicurvate leaf-like embossing dies.

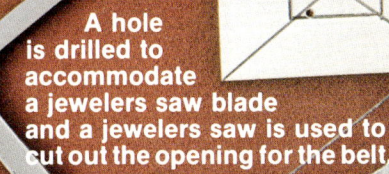

A hole is drilled to accommodate a jewelers saw blade and a jewelers saw is used to cut out the opening for the belt.

Male Die

Male Die

The female is struck first on the face of the buckle and then the male die is punched from the back forming the embossed design.

The buckles on the very early concha belts were quite small and rather inconspicuous compared with the conchas. After a few years, however, they were made as large or larger than the conchas. In some of the early photographs of Navajos around 1900, many larger buckles are shown being worn—some even alone on belts without conchas.

A piece of 14 gauge round wire is cut wider than the belt opening, the ends flattened and this bar is soldered across in the center of the underside of the belt opening.

The stones are selected, bezels are made and soldered on the buckle.

A tongue is made of a piece of 10 gauge ½ round silver wire bent round on one end to fit the cross bar and rounded on the other.

The stones are set and the buckle polished.

Stamps and Dies, courtesy of Tucker Tool Co., Prescott, Arizona.

THE BUTTERFLY SPACER

A piece of silver of 18 gauge thickness is cut to 1 x 2 inches and the center marked.

The butterfly spacer or belt slide is of unknown origin appearing in pictures of Navajo Indians wearing concha belts sometime after 1900. Its vertical lines make a striking contrast to the horizontal lines of the oval concha, and presents another element to give the artistic Indian mind full play.

The female die is stamped into the front side of the silver blank, forming a flower-like design.

A stamping die is used to complete the design.

The embossing is completed by hammering the male die into the reverse side of the blank.

The design is outlined and sawed out with a jewelers saw following the curvature of the stamping.

The butterflies shown outlining this picture are only a few of the many, many possible designs.

A copper belt hasp is made and soldered on the long way of the spacer.

The design is darkened, and the spacer buffed and polished.

28

THE NAVAJO CONCHA BELT

This unique and intriguing article of adornment appeared on the Navajo reservation sometime around 1870. It is probable that the belt was copied from a combination of the Mexican concha or button and the nickel silver plain domed belt concha which was usually a machine-manufactured item sold to the Indians of the east and central plains. The Navajo have taken the plain concha and added designs copied from the leather stamps of the Spanish and Moors and produced a beautiful article that is very Navajo. The concha belt is made and worn by many tribes other than the Navajo, especially the Pueblo Indians of the Southwest.

Made about 1910.

Made about 1925.

Made about 1895.

These are three old Navajo belts. The one in the center illustrates the use of male and female embossing dies on the buckle and butterflies. The large center rosette was embossed by the use of a male and female die. The two belts without the turquoise were made by all hand die stamping. The embossing was done by doming the conchas and the bicurvate designs on the buckles were done by hammering into a depression in a wooden block.

This belt was assembled using the pieces shown pictured in the three belt making series.

These three belts are contemporary, shown here to illustrate a variety of designs.

29

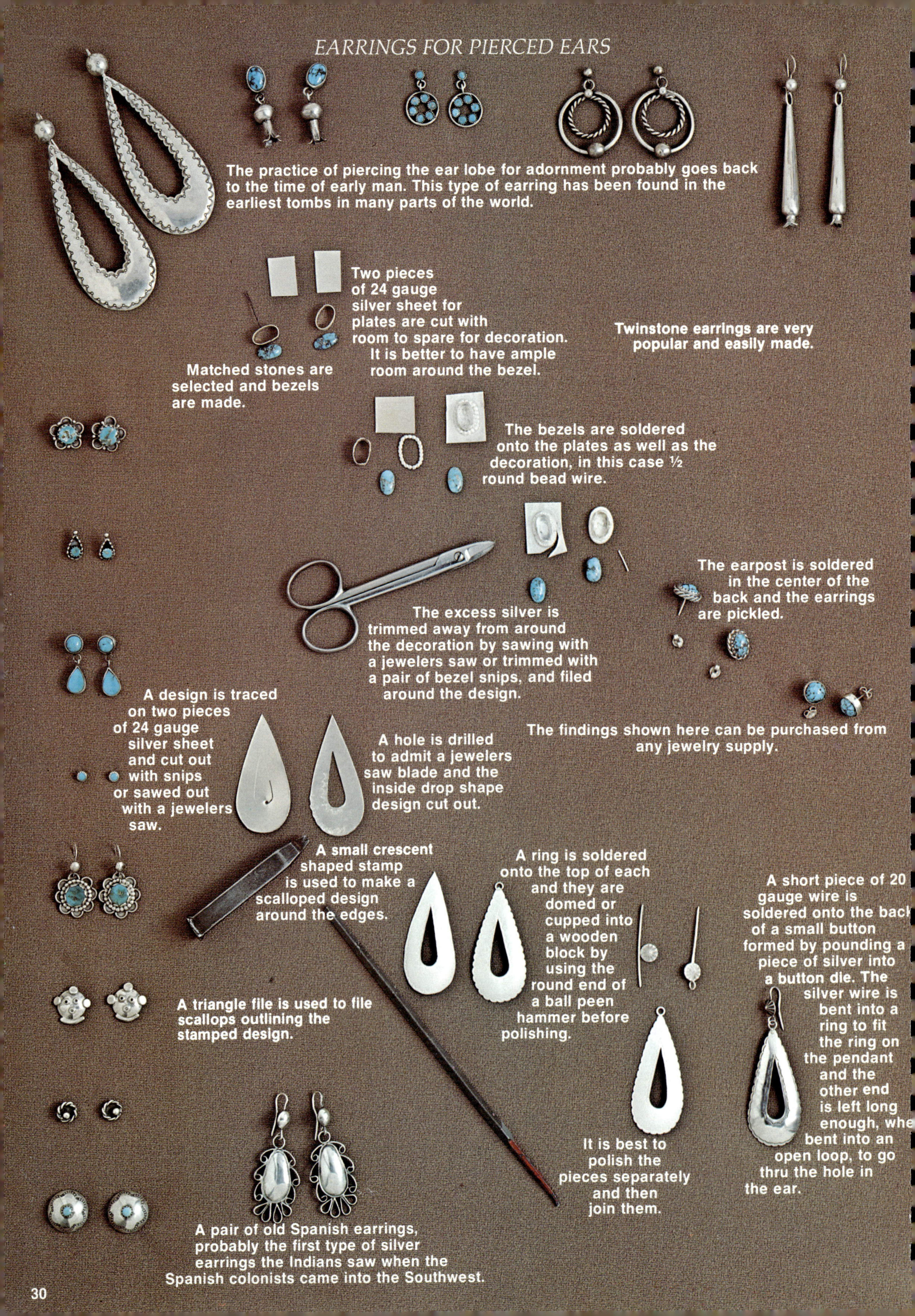

EARRINGS FOR PIERCED EARS

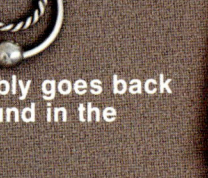

The practice of piercing the ear lobe for adornment probably goes back to the time of early man. This type of earring has been found in the earliest tombs in many parts of the world.

Two pieces of 24 gauge silver sheet for plates are cut with room to spare for decoration. It is better to have ample room around the bezel.

Matched stones are selected and bezels are made.

Twinstone earrings are very popular and easily made.

The bezels are soldered onto the plates as well as the decoration, in this case ½ round bead wire.

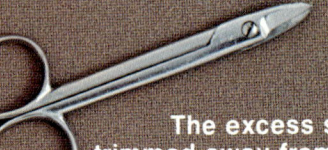

The earpost is soldered in the center of the back and the earrings are pickled.

The excess silver is trimmed away from around the decoration by sawing with a jewelers saw or trimmed with a pair of bezel snips, and filed around the design.

A design is traced on two pieces of 24 gauge silver sheet and cut out with snips or sawed out with a jewelers saw.

A hole is drilled to admit a jewelers saw blade and the inside drop shape design cut out.

The findings shown here can be purchased from any jewelry supply.

A small crescent shaped stamp is used to make a scalloped design around the edges.

A ring is soldered onto the top of each and they are domed or cupped into a wooden block by using the round end of a ball peen hammer before polishing.

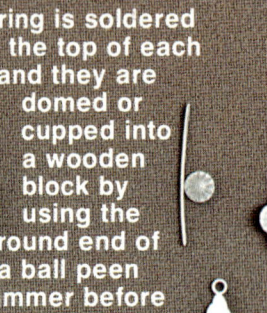

A short piece of 20 gauge wire is soldered onto the back of a small button formed by pounding a piece of silver into a button die. The silver wire is bent into a ring to fit the ring on the pendant and the other end is left long enough, when bent into an open loop, to go thru the hole in the ear.

A triangle file is used to file scallops outlining the stamped design.

It is best to polish the pieces separately and then join them.

A pair of old Spanish earrings, probably the first type of silver earrings the Indians saw when the Spanish colonists came into the Southwest.

THE EARSCREW EARRING

This type is essentially the same as the pierced but owes its holding power to pinching or squeezing the ear lobe by tightening a tiny screw device to make the earring stay on.

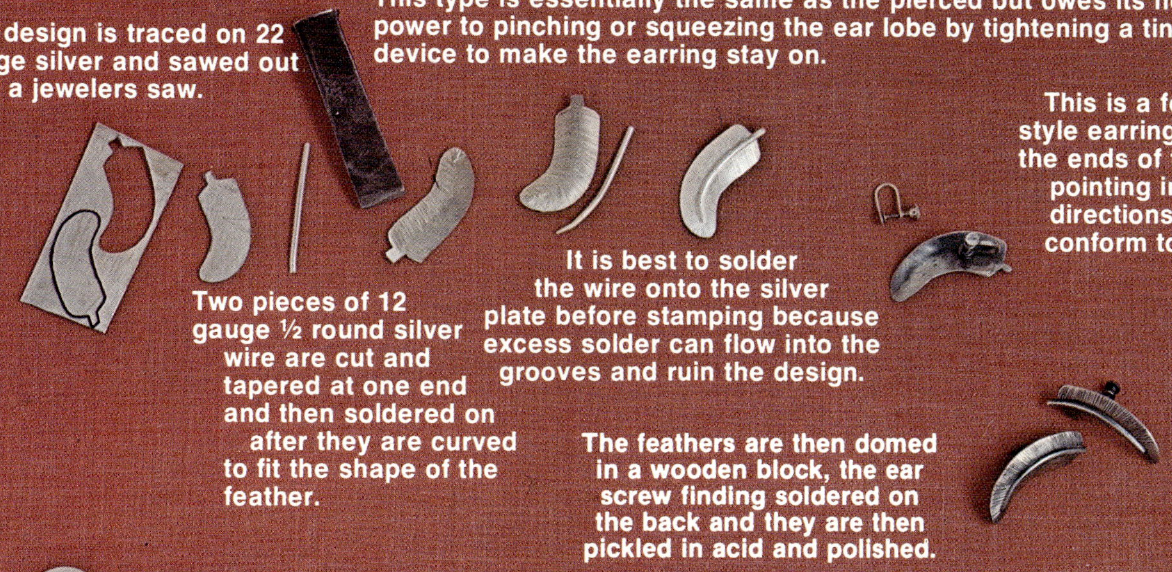

The design is traced on 22 gauge silver and sawed out with a jewelers saw.

Two pieces of 12 gauge ½ round silver wire are cut and tapered at one end and then soldered on after they are curved to fit the shape of the feather.

It is best to solder the wire onto the silver plate before stamping because excess solder can flow into the grooves and ruin the design.

This is a feather style earring with the ends of the feathers pointing in opposite directions to conform to each ear.

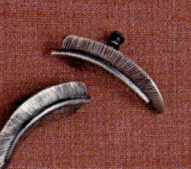

The feathers are then domed in a wooden block, the ear screw finding soldered on the back and they are then pickled in acid and polished.

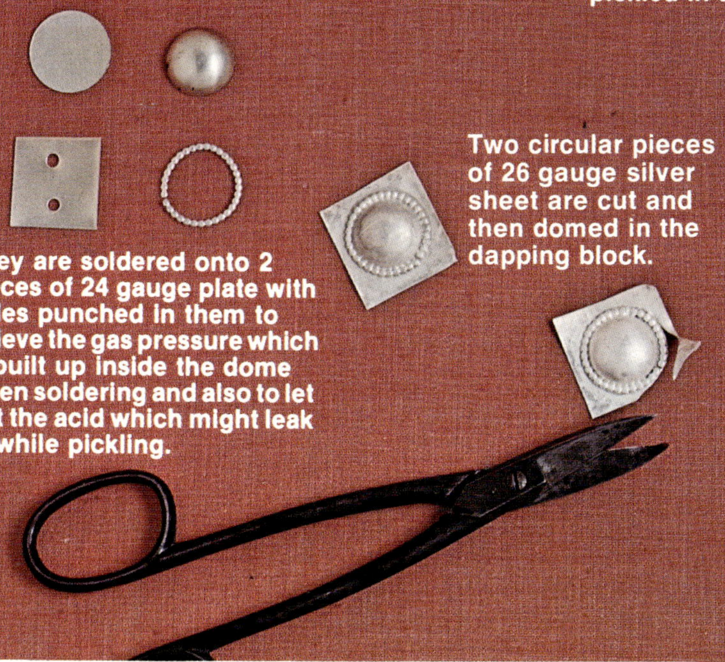

They are soldered onto 2 pieces of 24 gauge plate with holes punched in them to relieve the gas pressure which is built up inside the dome when soldering and also to let out the acid which might leak in while pickling.

Two circular pieces of 26 gauge silver sheet are cut and then domed in the dapping block.

A small band of ½ round bead wire is soldered around each dome and the excess silver is trimmed with curved snips or jewelers saw and filed.

The ear screw findings are soldered onto the backs and the earrings polished.

THE CLIP TYPE EARRING

This type earring uses a patented spring clip that grabs or pinches the earlobe.

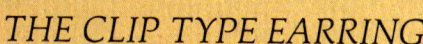
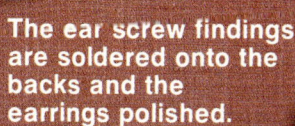

Here are several types available at jewelry supply stores. Two sizes are shown here both of sterling silver. They come in two parts, one to be soldered onto the earring and the other, the clip, is to be assembled after soldering by forcing the two pivot prongs into the holes of the other. More tension or grab can be provided by slightly bending the spring piece.

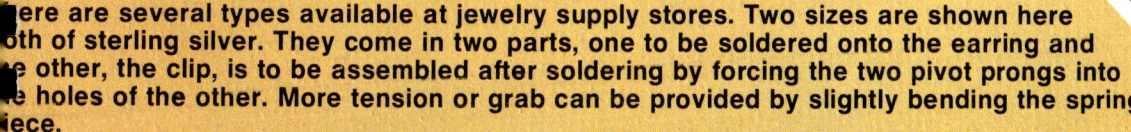

THE NAVAJO HATBAND

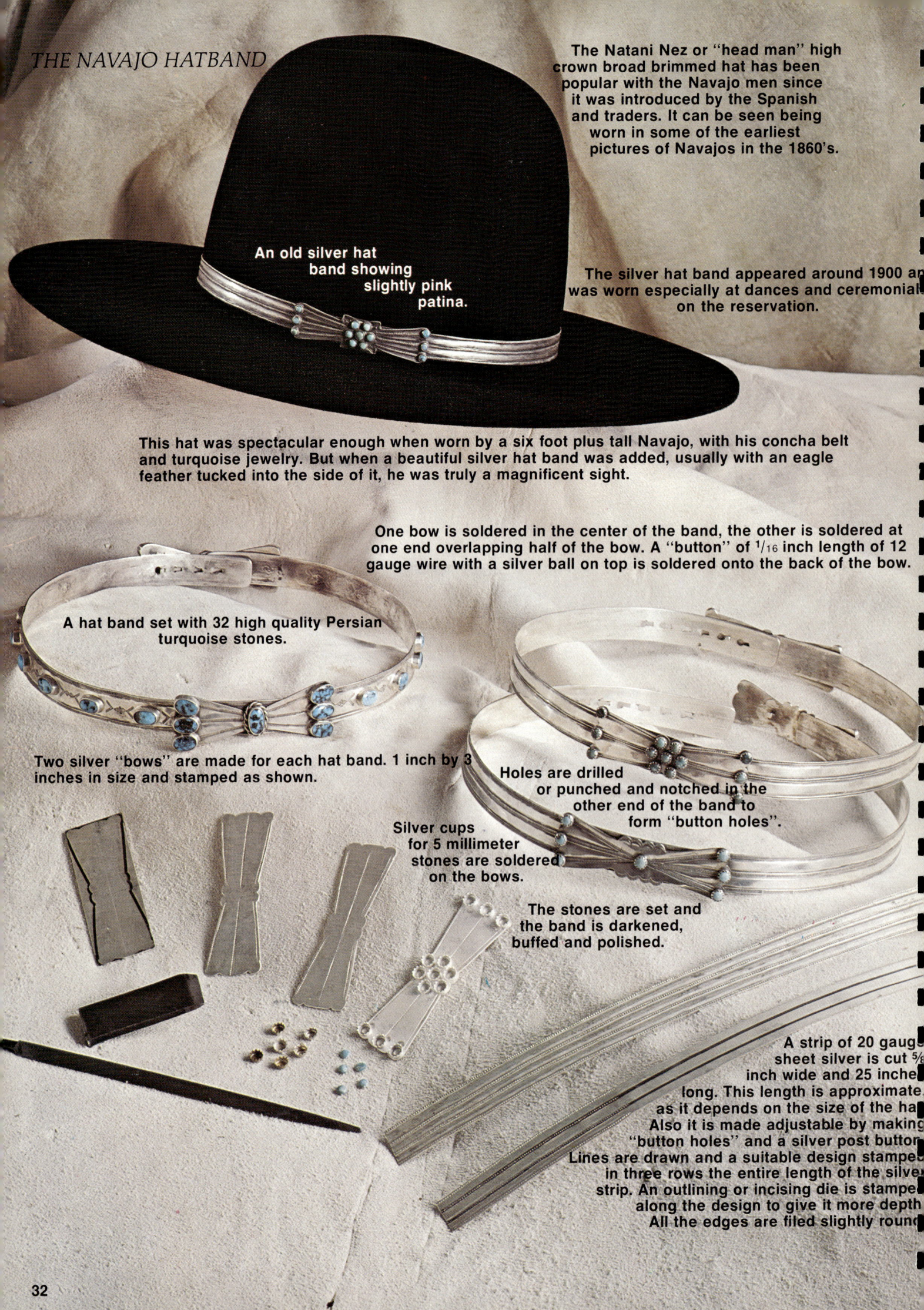

The Natani Nez or "head man" high crown broad brimmed hat has been popular with the Navajo men since it was introduced by the Spanish and traders. It can be seen being worn in some of the earliest pictures of Navajos in the 1860's.

An old silver hat band showing slightly pink patina.

The silver hat band appeared around 1900 and was worn especially at dances and ceremonials on the reservation.

This hat was spectacular enough when worn by a six foot plus tall Navajo, with his concha belt and turquoise jewelry. But when a beautiful silver hat band was added, usually with an eagle feather tucked into the side of it, he was truly a magnificent sight.

One bow is soldered in the center of the band, the other is soldered at one end overlapping half of the bow. A "button" of $1/16$ inch length of 12 gauge wire with a silver ball on top is soldered onto the back of the bow.

A hat band set with 32 high quality Persian turquoise stones.

Two silver "bows" are made for each hat band. 1 inch by 3 inches in size and stamped as shown.

Holes are drilled or punched and notched in the other end of the band to form "button holes".

Silver cups for 5 millimeter stones are soldered on the bows.

The stones are set and the band is darkened, buffed and polished.

A strip of 20 gauge sheet silver is cut $5/8$ inch wide and 25 inches long. This length is approximate as it depends on the size of the hat. Also it is made adjustable by making "button holes" and a silver post button. Lines are drawn and a suitable design stamped in three rows the entire length of the silver strip. An outlining or incising die is stamped along the design to give it more depth. All the edges are filed slightly round.

32

THE HOSTEEN CHARLIE HAT

This, the present day "cowboy" version of the Natani Nez hat, is worn by many of the young Navajos on or off the reservation. It is essentially the same as the old style Stetson body but blocked "cowboy" style with a top crease, sides pinched and swept brim. The young Indians prefer a concha type hat band or belt rather than the solid silver band, and also it is new and different.

A rectangular piece of 20 guage silver is cut 1 inch by 1-1/4 inch and the center is marked.

A hole is drilled to accommodate the jewelers saw blade and the 1/2 by 1/2 inch hole is cut and filed for the belt.

The design is stamped around the edge and scallops are filed outlining the design.

14 conchas and a buckle make up this hat belt but the number depends on the hat size and how closely they are spaced.

A one inch piece of 14 gauge silver wire is cut to make the cross bar and the ends flattened. This is soldered to the back of the buckle. A tongue is made from the same size piece of silver wire filed, and bent around the cross bar. The buckle is then darkened, buffed and polished.

A male and female oval button die is used to form the small conchas.

Here the same size blank is used for both the buckle and concha.

A design is stamped around the conchas and filed outlining the design.

Belt hasps are made from strips of 3/16 inch 22 gauge copper sheet bent around a 1/4 inch wide file.

The conchas are darkened, buffed, and polished, then strung onto the belt.

These are soldered to the back of the conchas. Copper is used because it is soft and when the concha is in place on the belt it can easily be mashed down, firmly holding the concha.

THE NAJA

Naja is the name of the pendant at the bottom of the squash blossom necklace. It is also worn in the center of the Navajo headstall or bridle.

The najas shown here are all made of triangle or 1/2 round wire about 5 gauge or larger, bent around a form or mandrel. They are all handwrought, not cast.

A wire bending jig

A 1-1/2 inch pipe coupling is welded to a piece of steel plate, a peg or screw is used to hold the wire while bending it several times around the pipe coupling.

The loops formed in this manner can be clipped apart and flattened on an anvil with a rawhide mallet.

The center or smaller one was hand shaped to fit inside the larger one.

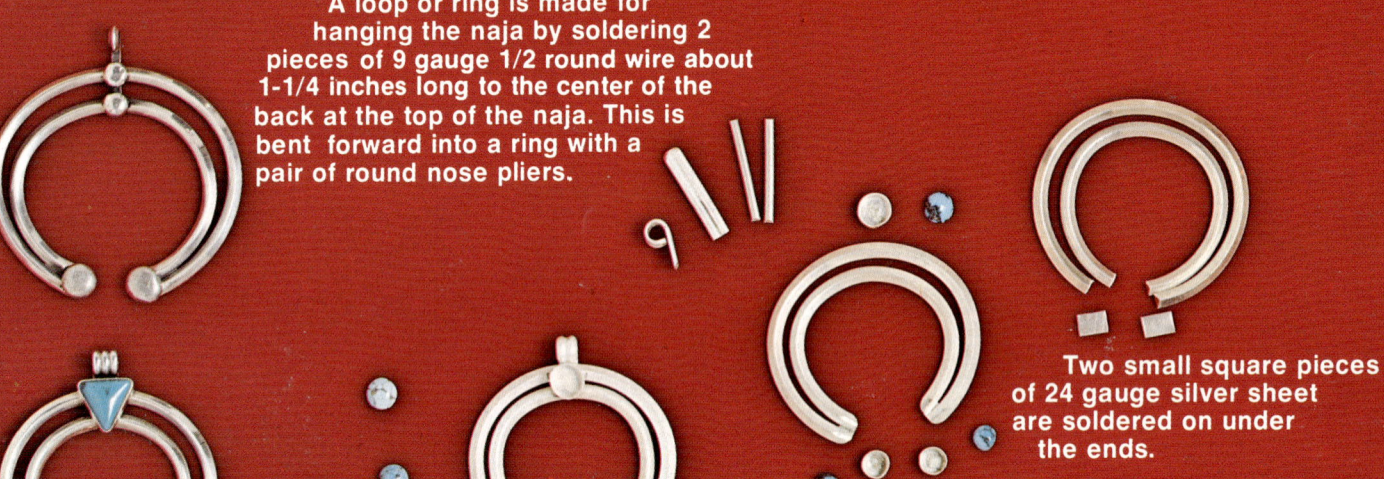

A loop or ring is made for hanging the naja by soldering 2 pieces of 9 gauge 1/2 round wire about 1-1/4 inches long to the center of the back at the top of the naja. This is bent forward into a ring with a pair of round nose pliers.

Two small square pieces of 24 gauge silver sheet are soldered on under the ends.

Cups are made, for the three stones, with bezels and plate and the cups are soldered on the front of the two loops at the ends and the top center.

Only a few of the many styles of najas are shown here, the designs of which can only be limited by the imagination.

The naja is darkened or antiqued, the stones are set and it is polished.

THE SQUASH BLOSSOM

It is very probable the Navajo copied the pomegranate blossom from the silver trouser ornaments of the Spanish, and it is fairly certain someone else applied the word squash blossom, because the Navajo called these ornaments, "Bead which spreads out."

9/16 inch discs of 28 gauge silver are cut for each blossom. When domed in a dapping block they are 1/8 inch smaller and form beads 7/16 inch in size. These edges of the halves are filed on a flat file so they fit together evenly. Holes are punched in each half with a small pointed punch. A strip of silver solder about 1/16 inch wide and longer than the bead is wide, is laid across one half of the bead, the other half bead is placed on top of the strip of solder as shown. Liquid flux is painted on, heat is applied and the halves soldered together.

A very attractive traditional style squash blossom necklace with a stamped design naja made from 18 gauge silver slightly domed.

The young pomegranates are shown here to illustrate the probability that the "squash blossom" is in reality a copy of a pomegranate blossom.

The small silver pomegranate is from Spain, the two larger ones are from Mexico.

An ancient and very worn squash or pomegranate blossom earring.

Three old Navajo silver "squash blossoms" of the 1880's.

The blossom end is cut from a piece of 24 gauge sheet silver. Three slits are cut and the blossom shaped with a pair of round nose pliers. A piece of 18 gauge silver is cut about 1/2 inch by 3/8 inch. A hole is drilled for stringing. The three pieces are wired together or held using a third hand device and all soldered together forming the blossom. Each blossom is pickled in acid, filed and polished.

35

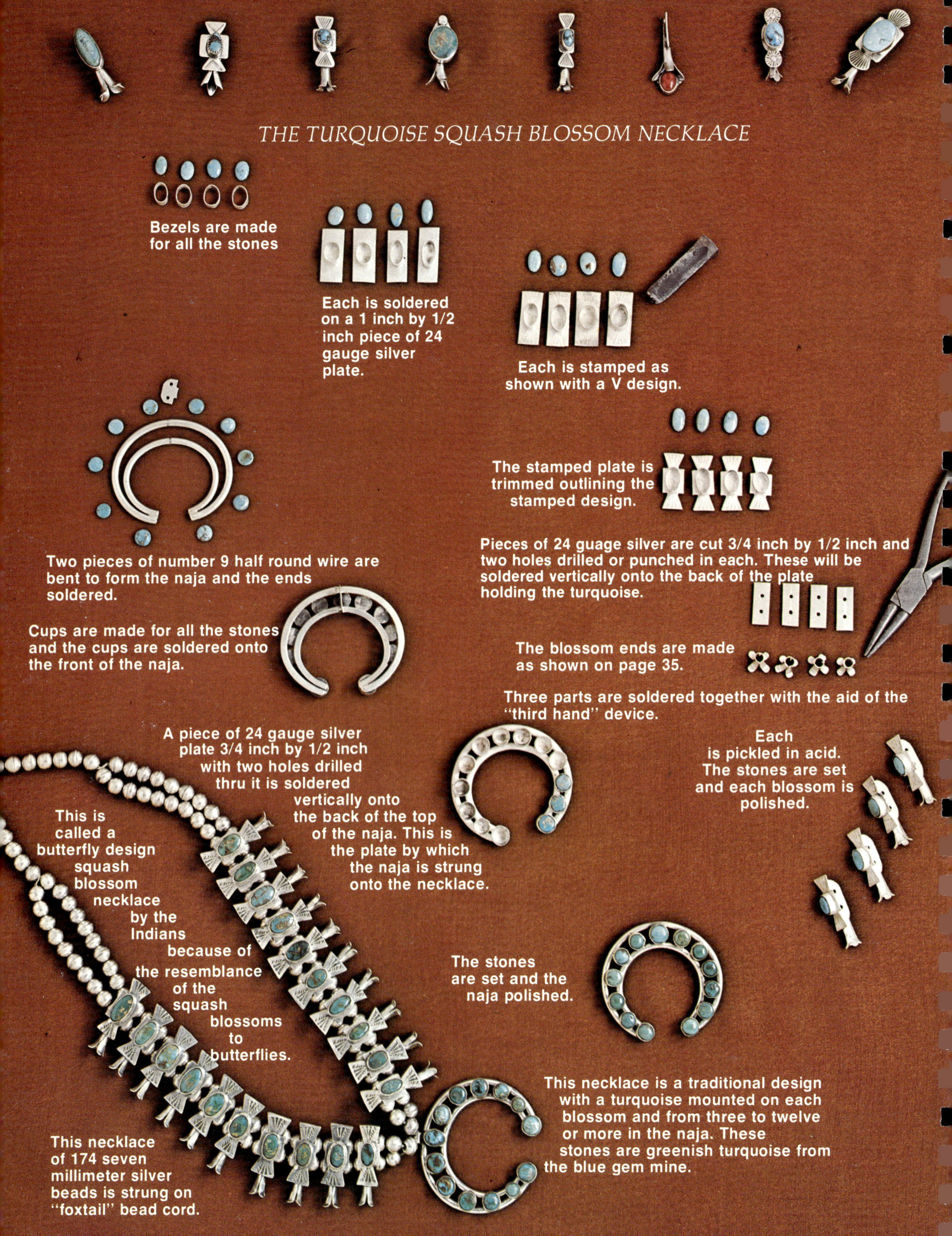

THE TURQUOISE SQUASH BLOSSOM NECKLACE

Bezels are made for all the stones

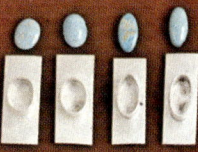

Each is soldered on a 1 inch by 1/2 inch piece of 24 gauge silver plate.

Each is stamped as shown with a V design.

The stamped plate is trimmed outlining the stamped design.

Two pieces of number 9 half round wire are bent to form the naja and the ends soldered.

Cups are made for all the stones and the cups are soldered onto the front of the naja.

Pieces of 24 guage silver are cut 3/4 inch by 1/2 inch and two holes drilled or punched in each. These will be soldered vertically onto the back of the plate holding the turquoise.

The blossom ends are made as shown on page 35.

Three parts are soldered together with the aid of the "third hand" device.

A piece of 24 gauge silver plate 3/4 inch by 1/2 inch with two holes drilled thru it is soldered vertically onto the back of the top of the naja. This is the plate by which the naja is strung onto the necklace.

Each is pickled in acid. The stones are set and each blossom is polished.

This is called a butterfly design squash blossom necklace by the Indians because of the resemblance of the squash blossoms to butterflies.

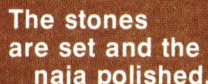

The stones are set and the naja polished.

This necklace of 174 seven millimeter silver beads is strung on "foxtail" bead cord.

This necklace is a traditional design with a turquoise mounted on each blossom and from three to twelve or more in the naja. These stones are greenish turquoise from the blue gem mine.

A squash blossom photographed at the University of Arizona Experimental Farm.

A Navajo naja covered with bluegreen turquoise from the Blue Gem Mine.

A turquoise covered necklace probably Zuni Indian made about 1920. It has a Navajo made clasp of unique stamped design.

A beautiful silver squash blossom necklace of the 1940's.

THE SQUASH BLOSSOM NECKLACE

A squash blossom necklace of Persian turquoise with no visible "blossoms" made about 1970.

This unique necklace was originated by the Navajo from three foreign elements. The silver beads were evidently evolved from two button halves soldered together to make a bead. The buttons were from Spanish clothing decoration. The "squash blossom" was evidently copied from the silver pomegranate blossom seen on the trousers of men from Granada, Spain. The naja or crescent shaped pendant was borrowed from the Spanish horse headstall or bridle which in turn was adopted from the Moors who probably got it by way of the Middle East, possibly from Mongolia. It was known in many early civilizations; the earliest are solid gold najas found in stone age graves in Ireland. Whatever the origins, the Navajo had the great ability to combine these elements into a beautiful piece of jewelry and the other Indians of the Southwest improved upon it.

A unique hand stamped naja displaying a free form cut turquoise, 1975.

An interesting type naja developed about 1925 and popular only for about a 10 year period.

37

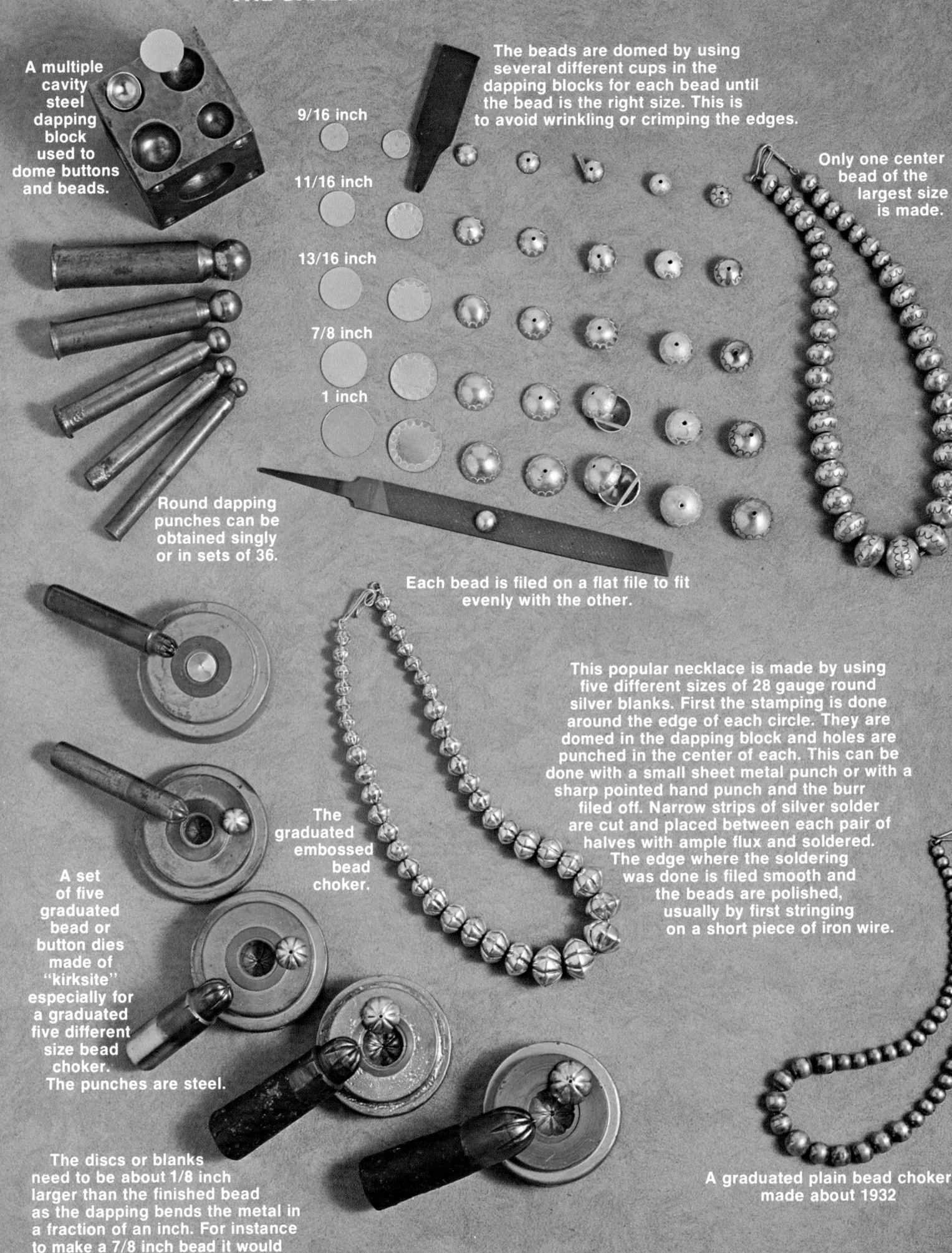

THE EMBOSSED BEAD CHOKER

The small button punch and die set is used to make these beads which results in a necklace of beads all the same size.

3/4 inch round discs are cut from 28 gauge silver sheet and punched into the button die. This results in beads about 5/8 inch in diameter. The cupped blanks are filed, the center hole is punched and the halves are soldered together. After pickling, the edges are filed and the beads are polished.

Certain styles of beads look better if tiny beads are strung between each of the larger beads. These small solid beads can be made by winding 9 gauge 1/2 inch round silver wire around a small nail and cutting them apart with a slitting saw and soldering the ends.

THE MELON BEAD NECKLACE

The melon bead was originally known as the melon seed bead.

Silver bead necklaces are usually strung on foxtail cord.

These elongated silver beads are made of 28 gauge silver strips punched into boat shaped cavities in a die with a punch of the same shape. This punch and die set is the same kind that is used to emboss and decorate many items of Navajo jewelry.

Silver solder in wire form.

After punching, the halves are trimmed usually with small snips, the edges filed flat and pairs soldered together. It is usually easier to solder these with wire solder. Just a touch to the fluxed and heated bead halves does it.

A melon seed bead necklace with small conical beads between each one.

THE WATCHBAND BRACELET

The silver band bracelet became the watchband bracelet by the substitution of the time piece for the center turquoise setting. This piece of jewelry has become very popular with men who sometimes hesitate to wear a bracelet.

A piece of 16 gauge silver sheet is cut 1-1/2 inches wide by 6 inches long, marked with the outline and sawed out with a jewelers saw.

Two pieces of 9 gauge 1/2 round silver wire are cut and bent to fit the outline and then soldered onto the silver plate.

Stones are selected and bezels made and the decorations are cut out. These are usually made of 22 or 24 gauge sheet.

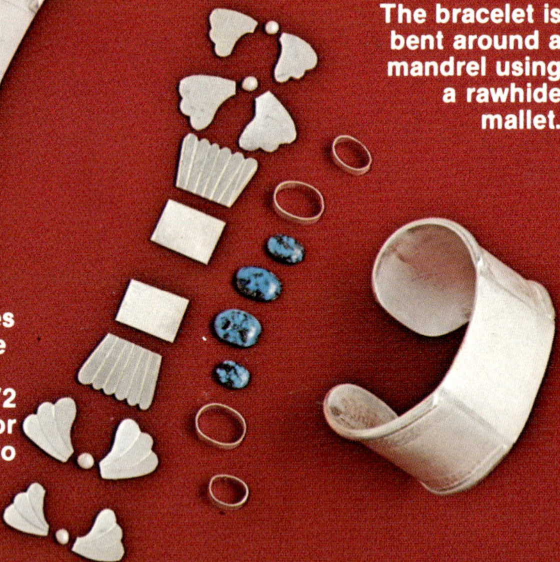

The bracelet is bent around a mandrel using a rawhide mallet.

Two pieces of 22 gauge silver sheet are cut slightly larger and stamped and filed. These pieces are bent over the watch pins after the watch is put on.

Two pieces of 24 gauge silver sheet 5/8 inch by 1/2 inch are cut for bending over to hold onto the watch pins.

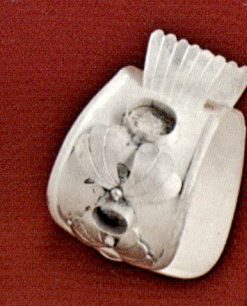

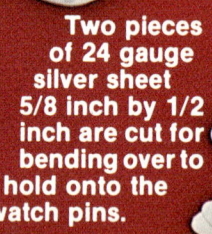

These two pieces are soldered vertically onto the band at the same time by holding with the "third hand," with a piece of 1/2 round silver wire as a spacer in between. Care should be taken to measure the size of the watch, so as to get these positioned correctly.

This stamp is used to make the curved design on the applique leaf.

The stones are set, the band is polished, the watch put on and the decoration carefully bent over the ends of the watch to hide the pins.

Courtesy of Tom Bahti Indian Arts, Tucson, Arizona

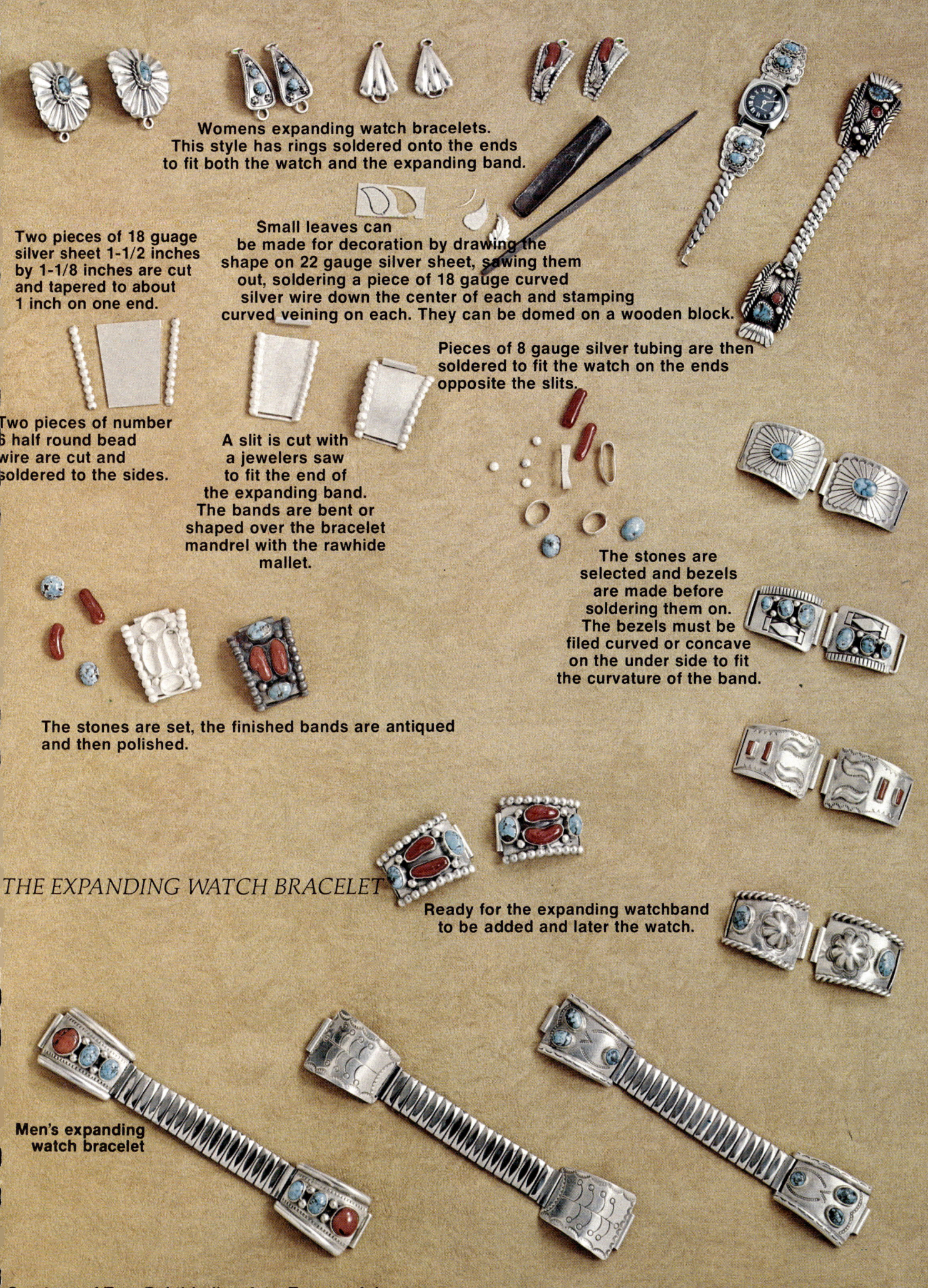

Womens expanding watch bracelets. This style has rings soldered onto the ends to fit both the watch and the expanding band.

Two pieces of 18 guage silver sheet 1-1/2 inches by 1-1/8 inches are cut and tapered to about 1 inch on one end.

Small leaves can be made for decoration by drawing the shape on 22 gauge silver sheet, sawing them out, soldering a piece of 18 gauge curved silver wire down the center of each and stamping curved veining on each. They can be domed on a wooden block.

Pieces of 8 gauge silver tubing are then soldered to fit the watch on the ends opposite the slits.

Two pieces of number 6 half round bead wire are cut and soldered to the sides.

A slit is cut with a jewelers saw to fit the end of the expanding band. The bands are bent or shaped over the bracelet mandrel with the rawhide mallet.

The stones are selected and bezels are made before soldering them on. The bezels must be filed curved or concave on the under side to fit the curvature of the band.

The stones are set, the finished bands are antiqued and then polished.

THE EXPANDING WATCH BRACELET

Ready for the expanding watchband to be added and later the watch.

Men's expanding watch bracelet

Courtesy of Tom Bahti Indian Arts, Tucson, Arizona.

THE SILVER PILL BOX

This strictly commercial item was made only on order from the trader.

Two pieces of 24 gauge sheet silver are cut 1-3/8 inches by 1-7/8 inches and notched at the corners.

 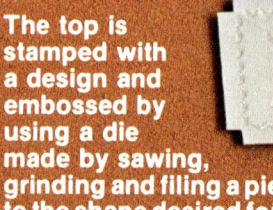

One should be cut slightly smaller than the other and bent slightly smaller to be the bottom.

The top is stamped with a design and embossed by using a die made by sawing, grinding and filing a piece of steel to the shape desired for the top.

The bottom is bent or formed in a vice over a hardwood block, cut to the correct size. The corners are soldered.

 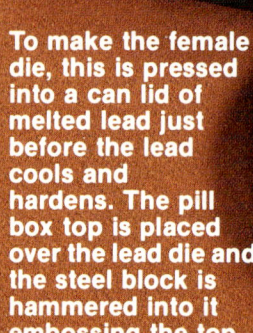 

Two short strips about 1/8 inch long of 12 gauge tubing are soldered on the back edge of the top. See Page 43.

To make the female die, this is pressed into a can lid of melted lead just before the lead cools and hardens. The pill box top is placed over the lead die and the steel block is hammered into it embossing the top.

Two pieces of 16 gauge wire are put through the pieces of tubing and bent V-shaped.

The edges are bent over the steel die and then soldered after it is removed from the die or form.

The box is pickled, antiqued, and polished.

The lid is put on the bottom or base of the box and the ends of the wires soldered to the bottom. Extreme care must be taken to only solder the ends of the wire to the box. If too much heat is applied, the wire will be soldered into the tubing and a lid that does not open will result.

Larger pill boxes for larger pills.

THE ROUND PILL BOX

This pillbox is designed around the small button or concha which is used as a top.

A piece of 18 gauge silver sheet is stamped in a male and female concha die to make a concha.

Scallops are filed outlining the design.

A small crescent punch is used to stamp a design around the ridges.

A strip of 24 gauge silver is cut 4-3/8 inches by 1 inch. This will be both the top and bottom sides of the box. The crescent design is stamped in three lines along the strip.

The strip for the top is then cut off the main piece.

The other or wider strip is bent around the mandrel and the ends soldered together forming a cylinder. This cylinder is soldered onto a plate of 24 gauge silver and the excess is trimmed off and filed.

This mandrel was made by pouring some melted white metal or die cast alloy into a piece of 1-3/8 inch gas pipe, 1-3/8 inches deep.

A stone is selected, a bezel made and soldered in the center of the concha.

The top strip is soldered into a ring shape and then soldered onto the underside of the concha.

A rim is made of thinner or 26 gauge silver about 1/8 inch wide and soldered into the large cylinder or base. This is the lip that will hold the lid in place. The lid should fit exactly but might take some little shaping.

A piece of 10 gauge tubing is soldered onto the rim of the lid as close to the edge as possible. A piece of 16 gauge wire is inserted into the tube and bent V-shaped. The two ends of the wire are soldered to the side of the base of the box.

The stone is set. The box antiqued and then polished.

Care should be taken to heat only the spot where the wires come in contact with the side of the box. If too much heat is applied, the wires could be soldered inside the tube and the lid would not open.

HAIR ORNAMENTS
COMBS — HAIRPINS — BARRETTES

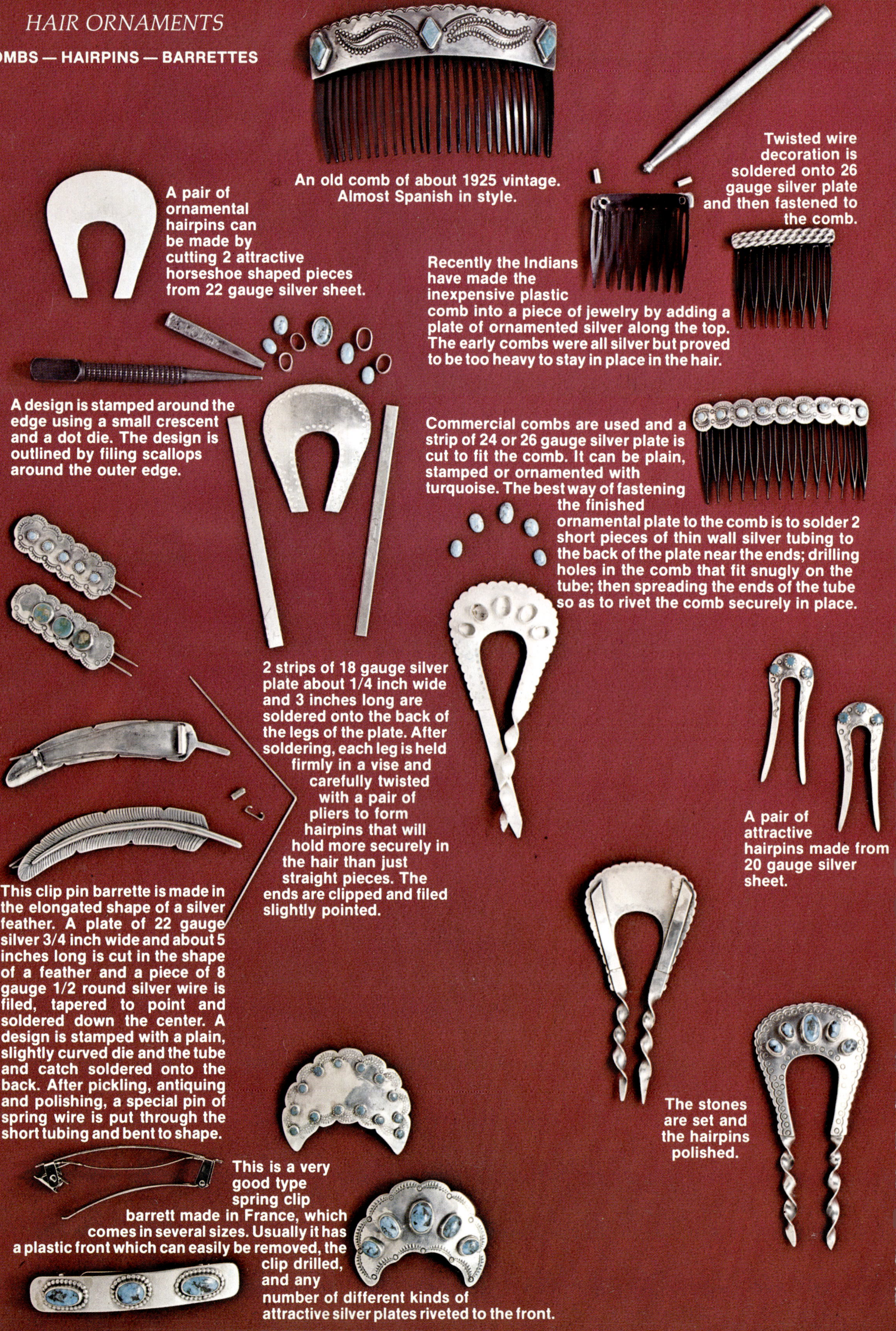

An old comb of about 1925 vintage. Almost Spanish in style.

A pair of ornamental hairpins can be made by cutting 2 attractive horseshoe shaped pieces from 22 gauge silver sheet.

Twisted wire decoration is soldered onto 26 gauge silver plate and then fastened to the comb.

Recently the Indians have made the inexpensive plastic comb into a piece of jewelry by adding a plate of ornamented silver along the top. The early combs were all silver but proved to be too heavy to stay in place in the hair.

A design is stamped around the edge using a small crescent and a dot die. The design is outlined by filing scallops around the outer edge.

Commercial combs are used and a strip of 24 or 26 gauge silver plate is cut to fit the comb. It can be plain, stamped or ornamented with turquoise. The best way of fastening the finished ornamental plate to the comb is to solder 2 short pieces of thin wall silver tubing to the back of the plate near the ends; drilling holes in the comb that fit snugly on the tube; then spreading the ends of the tube so as to rivet the comb securely in place.

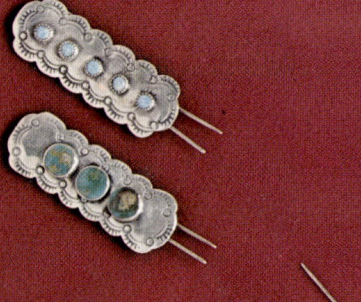

2 strips of 18 gauge silver plate about 1/4 inch wide and 3 inches long are soldered onto the back of the legs of the plate. After soldering, each leg is held firmly in a vise and carefully twisted with a pair of pliers to form hairpins that will hold more securely in the hair than just straight pieces. The ends are clipped and filed slightly pointed.

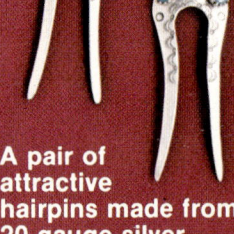

A pair of attractive hairpins made from 20 gauge silver sheet.

This clip pin barrette is made in the elongated shape of a silver feather. A plate of 22 gauge silver 3/4 inch wide and about 5 inches long is cut in the shape of a feather and a piece of 8 gauge 1/2 round silver wire is filed, tapered to point and soldered down the center. A design is stamped with a plain, slightly curved die and the tube and catch soldered onto the back. After pickling, antiquing and polishing, a special pin of spring wire is put through the short tubing and bent to shape.

The stones are set and the hairpins polished.

This is a very good type spring clip barrett made in France, which comes in several sizes. Usually it has a plastic front which can easily be removed, the clip drilled, and any number of different kinds of attractive silver plates riveted to the front.

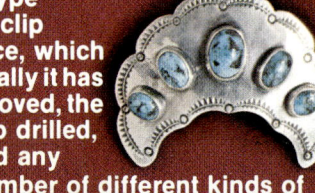

44

THE PONYTAIL CONE

A very attractive way to emphasize the beauty of a lovely hank of hair and also to keep it in place, is to wear a stamped and decorated split silver cone.

A 3-3/8 inch disk is cut from 26 gauge silver sheet. A 1 inch hole is cut below the center line so the top of the hole is slightly above center. A piece of silver is trimmed from the bottom of the disk below the hole making the hairpiece slightly flatter on the bottom.

DIANNE MAHAN

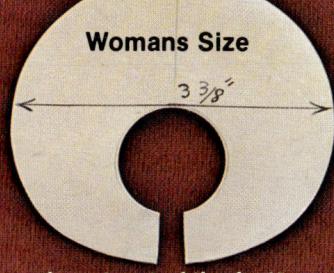

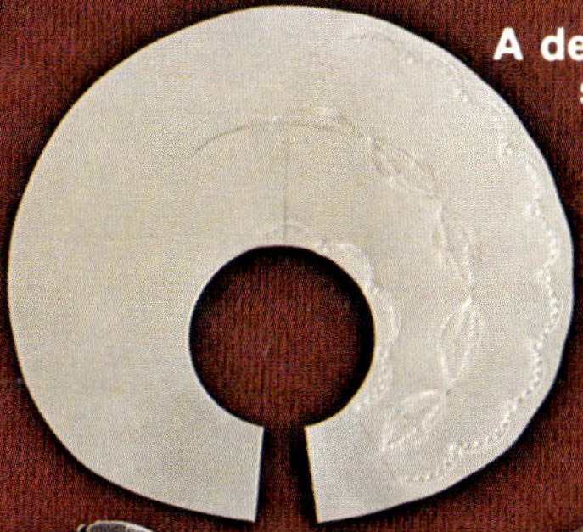

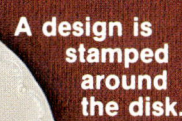

A design is stamped around the disk.

A piece is cut out of the bottom section about 1/4 inch wide to form a slot. The width of this slot determines the size of the hole to accommodate a large or small amount of hair. The larger the slot the smaller the hole and the steeper the shape of the cone when it is fastened around the hair.

A very attractive ponytail cone can be made by mounting a number of fine turquoise stones on it and the silver pin. The ponytail is usually bound or secured with a rubber band. The silver cone is slipped over the hair and "buttoned." The cone is then pushed up over or even with the rubber band and the pin inserted through the hair holding the cone in place.

Scallops are cut or filed outlining the stamped design.

Two holes are punched or drilled to accommodate a silver hairpin.

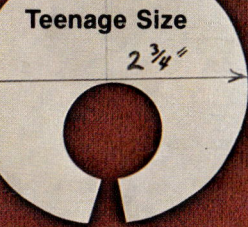

These are made by the same method as the larger, only the size is smaller.

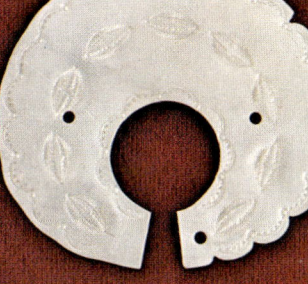

The third hole is to accommodate a button used for fastening the cone together when it is clasped around the hair.

The button is made by soldering a short piece of 14 gauge silver wire about 1/16 inch long and a silver ball on top of it onto the surface of the cone opposite the button hole.

A short slot is filed into the edge of the small hole towards the button to make the button hole.

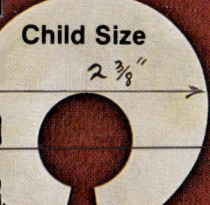

The design is darkened and the cone is polished.

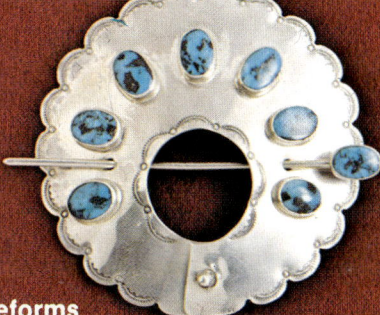

A pin is made from a four inch piece of 12 gauge silver wire with a silver ball soldered onto the end of it.

With thin gauge silver the work sometimes deforms around the stamping and needs to be occasionally flattened face down on an anvil with a rawhide mallet. Using thicker gauge silver usually makes the hair ornament too heavy.

THE BOLO TIE

The name is derived from the similarity to the Argentine bola or bolas throwning cord. It is frequently spelled bola but there is a definite feeling in the Southwest that it should be given its own distinct individual spelling, bolo.

THE MUDHEAD BOLO TIE
A 1-1/8 inch circle is cut and domed for the head. The torso, skirt and legs are cut and shaped by bending with round nose pliers and hammering into a wood block.

A piece of silver sheet 1-1/4 inches wide by 3-1/2 inches long is cut to use as a base.

All the silver sheet used in this figure is 24 gauge.

The bolo back is soldered on and the base is sawed away outlining the figure.

The bolo tie is another item of jewelry developed by the white man in the late 1940's and later adopted by the Indians.

The knobs on the head, the hands and feet are balls made from melted scrap. The arms are made from 2 gauge 1/2 round silver wire. The head, torso, legs, and skirt are all soldered onto the base at once. All the other pieces are progressively soldered on to complete the figure.

Attractive tips can be made like the buttons on page 12 by soldering a silver ring on top.

The base plate is the same size as above.

THE OWL KACHINA BOLO TIE
The base plate and most of the body pieces are made from 24 gauge silver.

All these parts are shaped and soldered onto the base including the arms and ruff made of 2 gauge 1/2 round wire which is around the neck. Two cups for the eyes and 3 bezels are soldered on for the turquoise stones.

After soldering on all the parts and the bolo back, the figure is cleaned and pickled; the base is sawed away outlining the figure. It is then polished.

Bolo tips and also necklace cones can be made by bending a V-shaped piece of 28 gauge silver sheet around the tapered end of a regular punch or nail set and then the joint soldered. A number of different bolo tips can be made by soldering on different kinds of beads with a silver ball on the tip. These tips are easily held on even without glue (rubber cement) by cutting or filing notches in the top end and crimping securely around the leather cord.

The bolo clip is put in and a braided leather cord is added with tips.

THE COLLAR CORNER

The Navajo collar corner is a dress decoration especially designed to be worn on the beautiful velvet blouse. It was inevitable the Indians should attractively decorate it with taste and beauty.

A pair of collar corners are made by cutting four pieces of 22 gauge silver 3/4 of an inch wide, 2 are cut 3 inches long and two 4 inches long. They are cut frame like and soldered together to match the angle of the particular collar.

A large curved die is stamped outlining the embosses and a small crescent die is stamped completely around the outside of each collar corner.

Five boat-like embosses are made by hammering the strips into a female die.

Six 5 millimeter cups are soldered on and 3 copper rings on the back of each.

The stones are set, the silver darkened and the collar corners are polished.

The velvet blouse is probably a direct descendant of the early Spanish velvet shirt, so admired and loved by the Navajo, it became a part of their traditional costume.

An attractive pair of collar corners on a lovely velvet blouse worn by Pamela Ray.

These are pairs of collar ornaments, probably the ancestor of the collar corners.

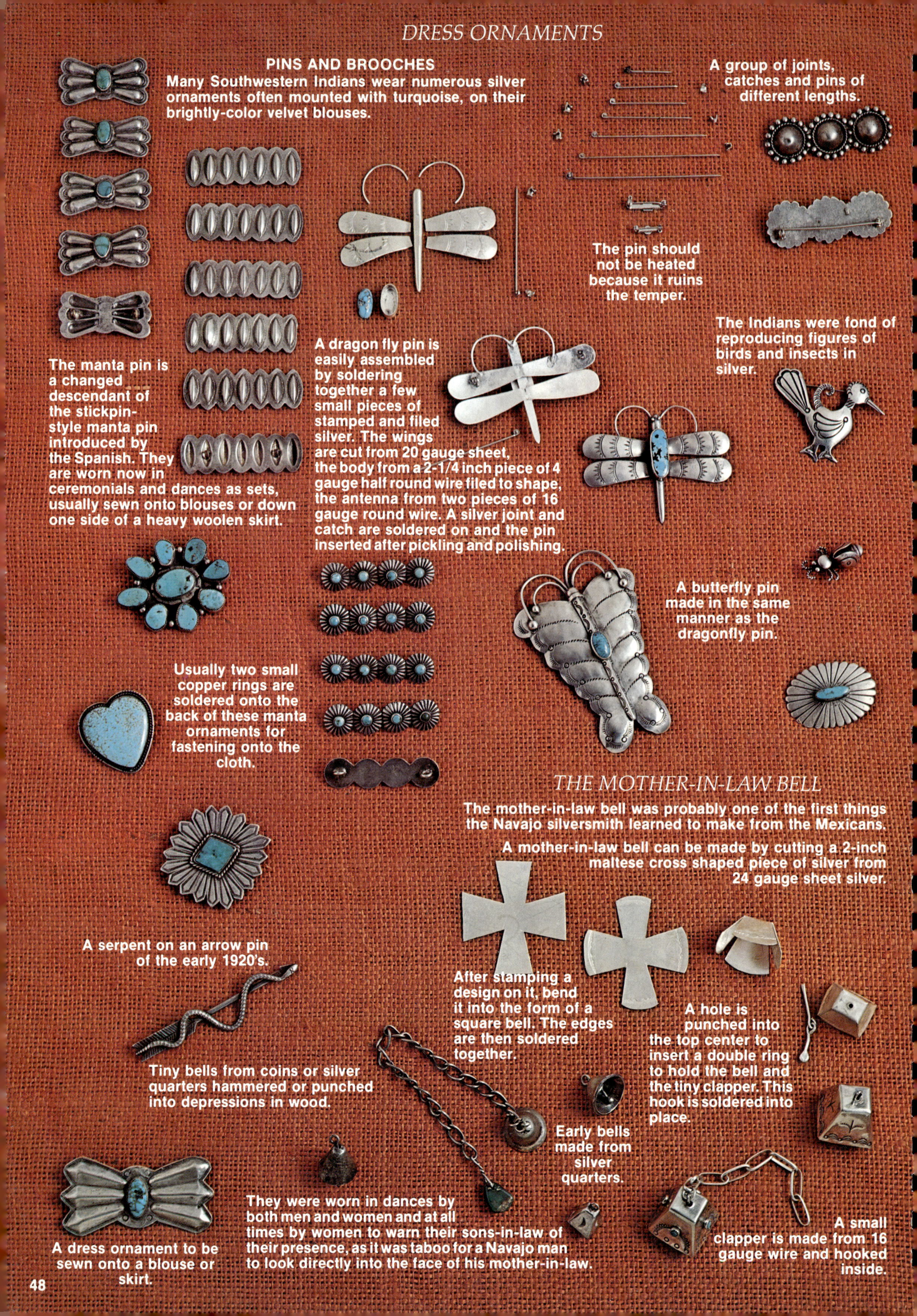

DRESS ORNAMENTS

PINS AND BROOCHES

Many Southwestern Indians wear numerous silver ornaments often mounted with turquoise, on their brightly-color velvet blouses.

A group of joints, catches and pins of different lengths.

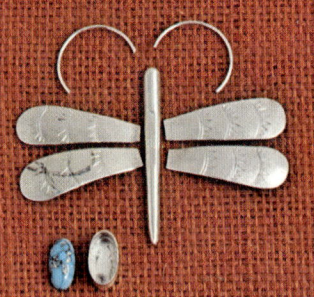

The pin should not be heated because it ruins the temper.

The manta pin is a changed descendant of the stickpin-style manta pin introduced by the Spanish. They are worn now in ceremonials and dances as sets, usually sewn onto blouses or down one side of a heavy woolen skirt.

A dragon fly pin is easily assembled by soldering together a few small pieces of stamped and filed silver. The wings are cut from 20 gauge sheet, the body from a 2-1/4 inch piece of 4 gauge half round wire filed to shape, the antenna from two pieces of 16 gauge round wire. A silver joint and catch are soldered on and the pin inserted after pickling and polishing.

The Indians were fond of reproducing figures of birds and insects in silver.

A butterfly pin made in the same manner as the dragonfly pin.

Usually two small copper rings are soldered onto the back of these manta ornaments for fastening onto the cloth.

THE MOTHER-IN-LAW BELL

The mother-in-law bell was probably one of the first things the Navajo silversmith learned to make from the Mexicans.

A mother-in-law bell can be made by cutting a 2-inch maltese cross shaped piece of silver from 24 gauge sheet silver.

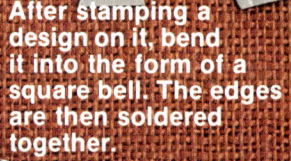

After stamping a design on it, bend it into the form of a square bell. The edges are then soldered together.

A hole is punched into the top center to insert a double ring to hold the bell and the tiny clapper. This hook is soldered into place.

A serpent on an arrow pin of the early 1920's.

Tiny bells from coins or silver quarters hammered or punched into depressions in wood.

Early bells made from silver quarters.

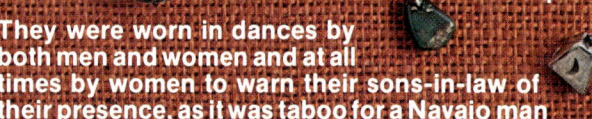

They were worn in dances by both men and women and at all times by women to warn their sons-in-law of their presence, as it was taboo for a Navajo man to look directly into the face of his mother-in-law.

A dress ornament to be sewn onto a blouse or skirt.

A small clapper is made from 16 gauge wire and hooked inside.

THE KETO OR BOW GUARD

The bowstring guard around the wrist for protection from the snap of the bowstring has been a companion to the archer since the invention of the bow.

All the Indians, but especially the Navajo have used this item as a subject for beautiful decoration since they learned how to work silver. At present archery is almost unknown among the Indians but the Keto has endured and gained great prominence as it is being worn ceremonially in almost all Southwestern Indian dances. Ketos probably lend themselves to the greatest variety of design more than any other item of Indian jewelry.

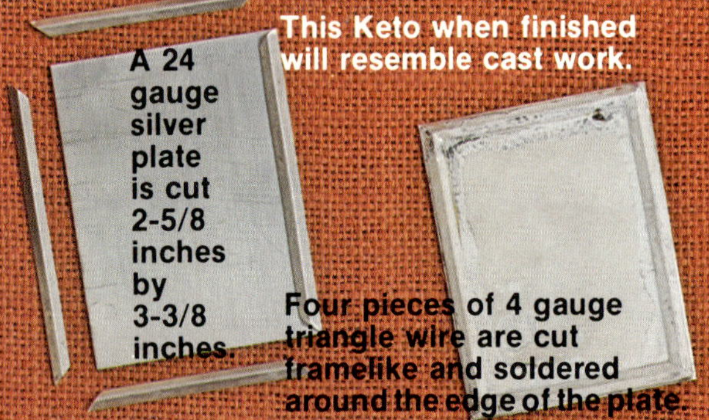

A 24 gauge silver plate is cut 2-5/8 inches by 3-3/8 inches.

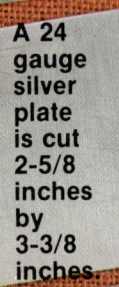

This Keto when finished will resemble cast work.

A jig is made by drilling a hole between two pieces of 1/4 inch by 1/2 inch wrought iron and clamping them in a vice, inserting individually the four 2 inch pieces of triangle wire and bending with large pliers into the S-shape or bicurvate floral elements of the design.

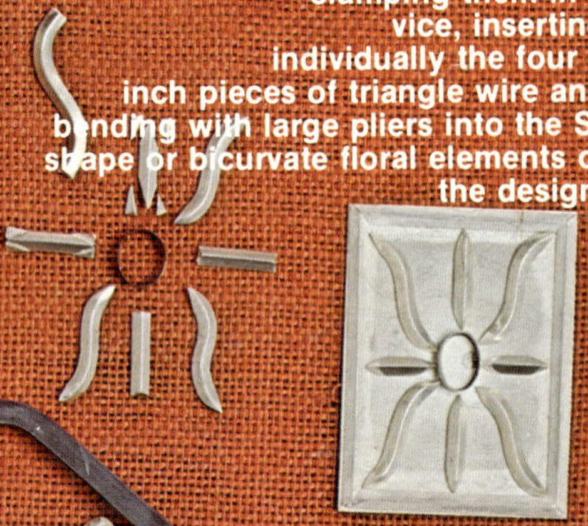

Four pieces of 4 gauge triangle wire are cut framelike and soldered around the edge of the plate. The ends are slightly flattened by hammering and then filed to a taper point. Four other short pieces of triangle wire are clipped or sawed boat shape and all eight fitted and soldered onto the plate, then cleaned in acid pickle.

A stone is selected and a bezel is made which is soldered in the center of the plate.

The Keto is slightly curved by hammering over a bracelet mandrel.

After pickling, the stone is set and the Keto polished.

Four U-shaped pieces of 16 gauge copper wire are soldered vertically, one at each corner of the back of the Keto.

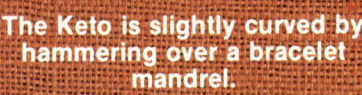

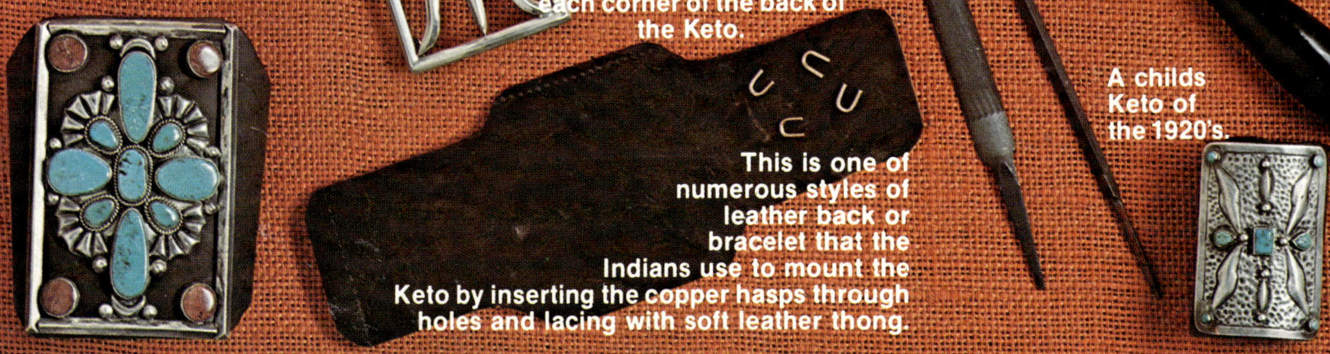

The plate is pierced and all background sawed out.

This is one of numerous styles of leather back or bracelet that the Indians use to mount the Keto by inserting the copper hasps through holes and lacing with soft leather thong.

A childs Keto of the 1920's.

50

THE NAVAJO TOBACCO CANTEEN

The Navajo canteen is probably descended from the Mexican rawhide canteen. And later, these were made by Navajo silversmiths for some members of the U.S. Cavalry, copying the old cavalry canteen for carrying tobacco and snuff.

Two old Mexican rawhide canteens still showing some decoration.

Two 2-1/2 inch discs of 24 gauge silver are cut and stamped with a design.

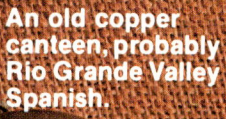

An old copper canteen, probably Rio Grande Valley Spanish.

The discs are then hammered into a shallow round cavity in a lead block by using a wooden mallet.

The edges of the two domed halves are filed flat to fit closely together. They are soldered by placing long flat pieces of solder between them and heating evenly all around.

A brass canteen, a miniature of the early U.S. cavalry canteen.

The spout is made with a piece of 22 gauge silver sheet, 3/4 inch by about 1 inch and soldered together after shaping on a mandrel. The tube thus formed is inserted in the round hole and soldered. Another tube is made slightly larger than the spout with a round top and a ring, to form the cap.

A spot of about 3/4 inch long is left unsoldered. This is expanded to fit the spout by forcing round nose pliers into the slit between the halves and twisting.

A silver canteen showing engraved cornstalk design.

The canteen is antiqued and polished.

A twisted wire is bent around the outside edge, wired in place and soldered. A ring is also soldered on the edge to hold a chain.

51

SILVER CASTING

Using a torch for melting the silver in a ceramic crucible.

In some molds a piece of fine binding wire can be shaped around the design to make the silver thicker and have a more perfect cast.

The design is marked on one face and then carved into the surface. A gate or channel must be cut in both surfaces to act as a funnel for the liquid metal. The surface of both molds is heated and smoked or covered with a layer of carbon or soot.

A Naja mold which has produced a large number of castings.

The silver should look like this just before pouring.

The excess silver is then sawed off and the casting filed and polished.

The polished Naja.

A sufficient quantity of silver is melted in a crucible to a very liquid state using a pinch of Borax to clean the surface of impurities while melting.

The melted silver must be poured in one continuous stream into the mold. The torch should be directed on the metal during the pouring to keep it from even slightly cooling.

The halves are clamped or bound together with wire.

The Navajo cast silver ornaments by making a two-piece stone mold of tuff or tufa which is found in many places on the reservation. Two pieces are cut with knives, files or a hack saw large enough to accommodate the object to be cast and from 1/2 inches to 2 inches thick. They are flattened on the faces first with a file or rasp and then by rubbing together until they fit perfectly.

A filed buckle ready for polishing.

A belt buckle mold

A rough cast.

The impressions of Indian designs around the borders were made by stamps belonging to a number of early silversmiths.

MAKING STEEL STAMPS
ANNEALING AND MAKING STEEL WORKABLE

Undoubtedly the most prized of all the tools of the Indian silversmith were his punches used to stamp designs on silver. They were a matter of pride even more so because he made them himself. They were almost always made from old tools, especially old files that had to be first softened or annealed in order to work them and then rehardened and tempered to spring hardness so they would resist chipping and breaking. These tools were copied from the Mexican leather stamps but had to be harder and stronger in order to stamp silver.

Pieces of files being heated to "cherry" red in a hollowed out piece of fire brick.

This is one way to anneal pieces of steel.

Annealing or softening of steel is done by heating it very hot and cooling it very slowly.

Pieces of steel being placed under plaster or lime for cooling.

Old files were usually broken into three pieces by clamping in a vice with about three inches of file protruding above the vice jaws. A cloth was wrapped around this portion in case a piece flew off. This third was broken off by striking with a hammer and was repeated with the other third. The ends were ground square on an emery wheel, then softened by heating to a cherry red and covered with plaster or lime for several hours to let the steel cool very slowly.

The softened and cooled piece is tested with an old file to see if it is really soft.

Four steps in making a stamp.
The end of a half round file is flattened and trued or made 90 degrees to the long axis of the stamp. The shape of the curve is filed on the outside with a flat file and on the inside with a half round file. Eleven small notches are filed on the inside curve with a tiny round needle file. Then a number 1 checkering file is used to file the tiny serrations in the outside curve.

A triangle file is flattened on the end. A small triangle file is used to file a notch, making a V-shaped punch. Serrations are made on the outside of the V with a number 1 checkering file.

A piece of round file is filed flat or trued on the end and a small punch is used to mark the center. A 3/16 inch hole is drilled in the end about 1/16 inch deep. A tiny slitting file is used to file the serrations around the outside edge.

54

There are 358 shown here and it was unusual for any silversmith to have more than 50.

HARDENING AND TEMPERING STEEL STAMPS

Steel stamps are hardened by heating to a cherry red and quenching them in water with a quick circular or stirring motion so the entire piece of steel is quickly cooled by water circulation. They are cleaned with emery paper and are then heated to a certain color and quenched in water to relax the tension in the steel and make them tougher and less likely to chip or break when hammered. This is called tempering.

The colors of tempered steel:
Straw, very hard, will scratch glass;
Amber, hard as knife blade;
Purple, cold chisel hard;
Deep Blue, clock spring hard.

These are about the correct color for quick quenching in water to harden them.

Three hardened stamps after being cleaned with emery paper are placed on a piece of steel plate and the heat applied from underneath with a Prest-O-Lite torch.

Purple Medium Hard
Blue Spring Hard
Amber Hard
Straw Very Hard

A checkering file and a half round file.

As the punches get hotter the steel will oxidize and turn the color of the temper. The color indicates the hardness and the punch should be plunged into water the instant this color is reached. Indian stamps for silver should be amber or purple.

An old file is used to test if the stamp is hard before tempering.

A group of needle files.

If it does not cut and slides over the surface of the stamp it is hard and can be tempered. If the file cuts or scratches it then, it is soft and should be reheated and quenched again to harden.

Five steps in making a punch: A half round piece of file is flattened 90 degrees to the long axis. The outside of the crescent filed. A sharp crescent stamp is driven into the stamp with a blow of the hammer. Serations are filed on the inside with a small triangle needle file. Serations are filed on the outside of the crescent with a number 1 checkering file. The stamp is now ready for hardening and tempering.

Two nail set punches used to make circles or dots on silver.

A long thin crescent stamp can be made from a flat file by filing the outside crescent shaped, then filing the inside with a half round file and filing the serations on the outside of the crescent with a checkering file.

55

HOPI STYLE OVERLAY

Hopi overlay design jewelry is essentially a heavy piece of silver plate with the design cut out and soldered on top of a thinner solid plate of silver, making a negative design which is usually textured and darkened.

Three Hopi overlay pieces of jewelry with designs taken from pottery and basketry motifs.

This belt buckle is made of two pieces of silver plate 2-1/4 by 3 inches in size; one of 20 gauge and the other 22 gauge.

This distinct style or technique of making jewelry is popularly called Hopi overlay and was developed by several Hopi silversmiths sometime around 1940. The Hopi do not limit themselves to this style and of course, overlay is done by many Indian silversmiths other than the Hopi.

A badger paw print is drawn in black ink on the 20 gauge plate. A hole is drilled in each blackened segment of the design and each cut out with a jewelers saw.

A Hopi ring of stylized hand design.

A number of pieces of silver solder are melted with ample flux onto the reverse side of this plate and then it is pickled and cleaned. Fresh flux is applied and the two plates soldered together. This is best accomplished by placing the two pieces with the cut out piece on top using ample flux, on a woven wire soldering frame, heating evenly by alternating the torch flame from top to bottom until the solder flows completely around the edges of the design and the outer edges of the plates so the two are firmly welded together.

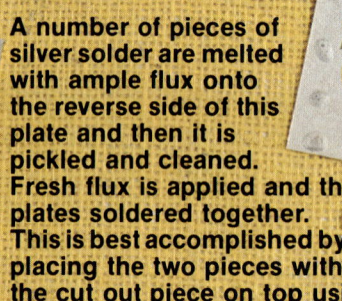

A commercial buckle back and peg are soldered onto the back of the buckle.

A small line embossing tool is used to texture the entire cut out design. Practice texturing on a piece of scrap silver before trying to do it on the buckle.

A bezel is made for a small round turquoise stone and soldered onto the buckle as shown. The corners of the buckle are rounded and all edges are filed smooth. The buckle is slightly curved or bent around a bracelet mandrel.

Two pieces of 18 gauge silver wire are bent to shape, forming a design, and soldered into the center cut out. The top of the wire is filed smooth.

A Hopi overlay link watch bracelet with spiderweb turquoise

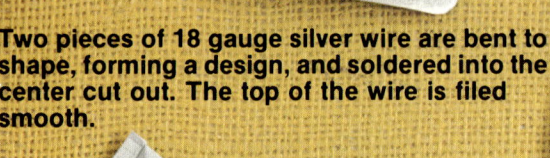

This style crushed turquoise jewelry was made popular in recent times by several members of the Singer family.

The stone is set, the buckle is polished and then the design is carefully darkened with Hil-ox antiquing fluid using an iron wire.

The construction is very similar to the Hopi overlay techniques. After the piece of overlay is finished except for polishing, the crushed fragments are placed in the cut out design. Bits of coral and jet are also frequently used.
A liquid type epoxy is dropped over the stone fragments and allowed to penetrate. After hardening, the stone chips are cut down even with the surface of the silver, sanded, and polished.

A Hopi overlay money clip.

A Hopi pin incorporating a free form cut turquoise.

56

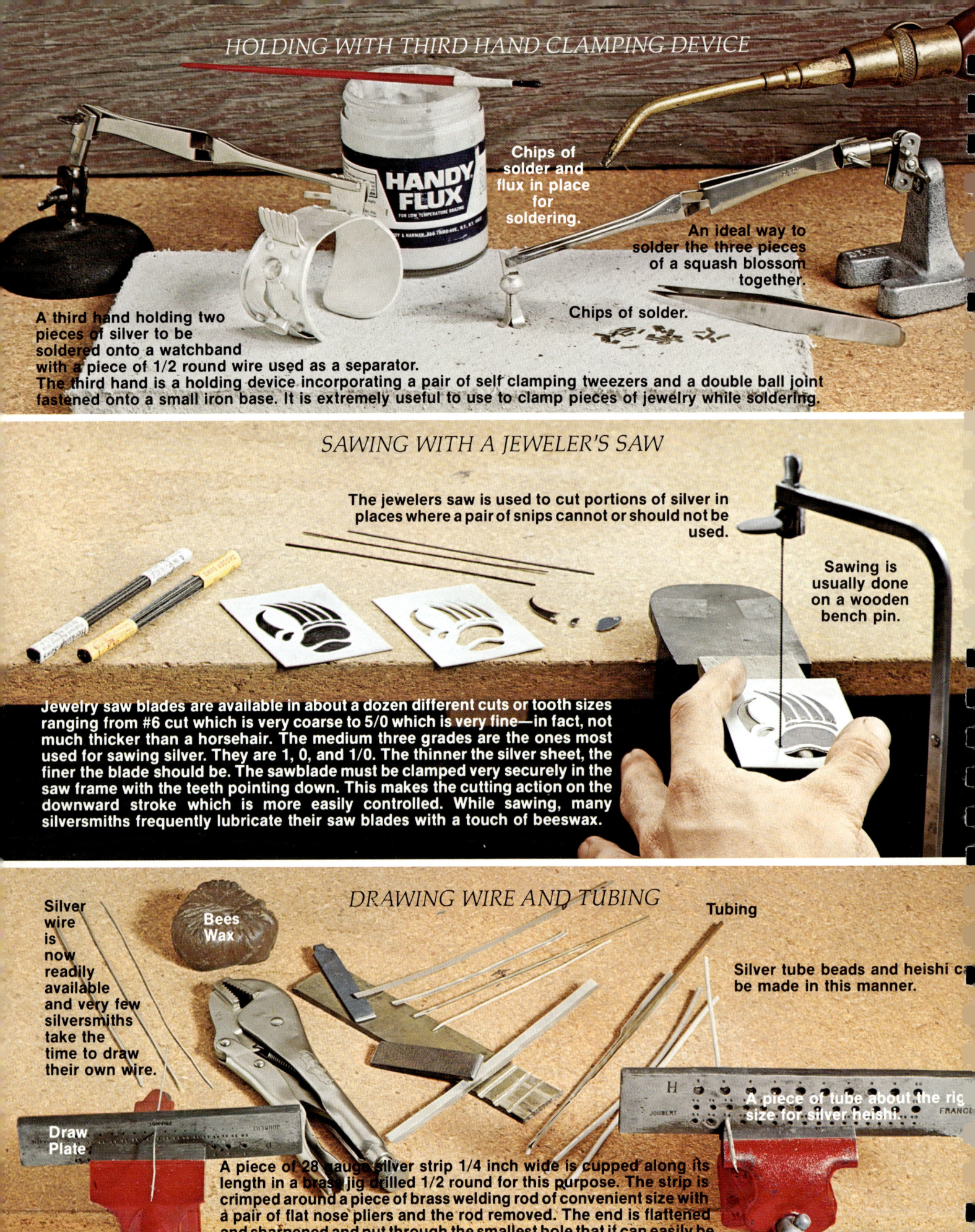

HOLDING WITH THIRD HAND CLAMPING DEVICE

Chips of solder and flux in place for soldering.

An ideal way to solder the three pieces of a squash blossom together.

Chips of solder.

A third hand holding two pieces of silver to be soldered onto a watchband with a piece of 1/2 round wire used as a separator. The third hand is a holding device incorporating a pair of self clamping tweezers and a double ball joint fastened onto a small iron base. It is extremely useful to use to clamp pieces of jewelry while soldering.

SAWING WITH A JEWELER'S SAW

The jewelers saw is used to cut portions of silver in places where a pair of snips cannot or should not be used.

Sawing is usually done on a wooden bench pin.

Jewelry saw blades are available in about a dozen different cuts or tooth sizes ranging from #6 cut which is very coarse to 5/0 which is very fine—in fact, not much thicker than a horsehair. The medium three grades are the ones most used for sawing silver. They are 1, 0, and 1/0. The thinner the silver sheet, the finer the blade should be. The sawblade must be clamped very securely in the saw frame with the teeth pointing down. This makes the cutting action on the downward stroke which is more easily controlled. While sawing, many silversmiths frequently lubricate their saw blades with a touch of beeswax.

DRAWING WIRE AND TUBING

Silver wire is now readily available and very few silversmiths take the time to draw their own wire.

Bees Wax

Tubing

Silver tube beads and heishi can be made in this manner.

A piece of tube about the right size for silver heishi.

Draw Plate

A piece of 28 gauge silver strip 1/4 inch wide is cupped along its length in a brass jig drilled 1/2 round for this purpose. The strip is crimped around a piece of brass welding rod of convenient size with a pair of flat nose pliers and the rod removed. The end is flattened and sharpened and put through the smallest hole that it can easily be pushed through. It is then lubricated with beeswax and the sharp end put through the next smallest hole and clamped with a pair of vise grip pliers and pulled through. This is repeated until the edges come together. Tubing made in this way can be soldered and pulled smaller after pickling. If the pulling gets too hard the tube or wire should be annealed or softened by heating to a red heat and pickling before proceeding.

BENDING A BRACELET

A bracelet mandrel of cast steel is a very useful tool to the silversmith. This one is mounted on a wooden 2 by 6 bolted to the bench and shaped to fit the inside of the mandrel. Many other shaping and bending jobs can be accomplished on this tool.

A bracelet is being shaped by hammering or tapping it just off the center so it bends the bracelet gradually around the mandrel. This must be reversed to shape the other side of the bracelet.

After Bending

Before Bending

DETERMINING THE SIZE OR GAUGE OF SILVER WIRE OR SHEET:

The American standard wire gauge for non-ferrous metals is used to find the size and thickness of mill run shapes of silver, copper, brass, and aluminum. The pieces inserted in the gauge slots illustrate the correct way to determine the size of the sheet or wire.

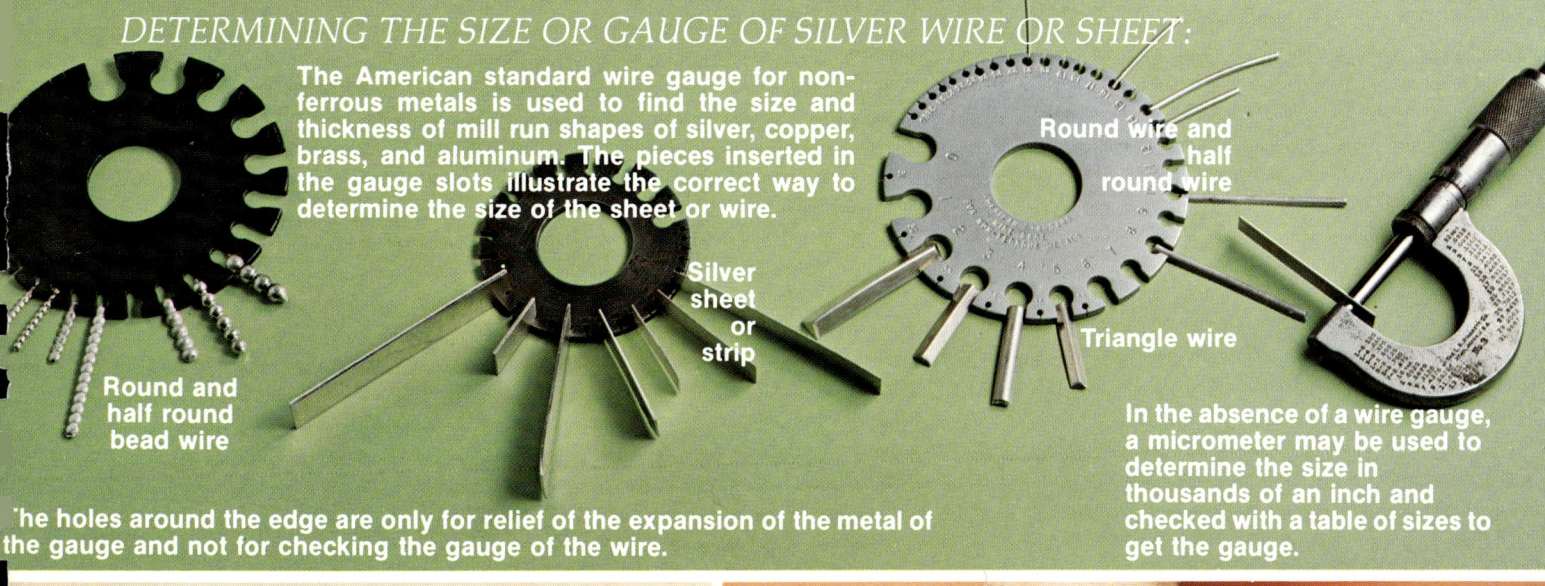

Round and half round bead wire

Silver sheet or strip

Round wire and half round wire

Triangle wire

In the absence of a wire gauge, a micrometer may be used to determine the size in thousands of an inch and checked with a table of sizes to get the gauge.

The holes around the edge are only for relief of the expansion of the metal of the gauge and not for checking the gauge of the wire.

STAMPING TRIANGLE WIRE

The problem of stamping a design on triangle wire is solved by cutting a triangle shaped slot with a hack saw in a piece of railroad track.

The slot should be cut so one face of the triangle wire is flat while stamping, which makes one face vertical.

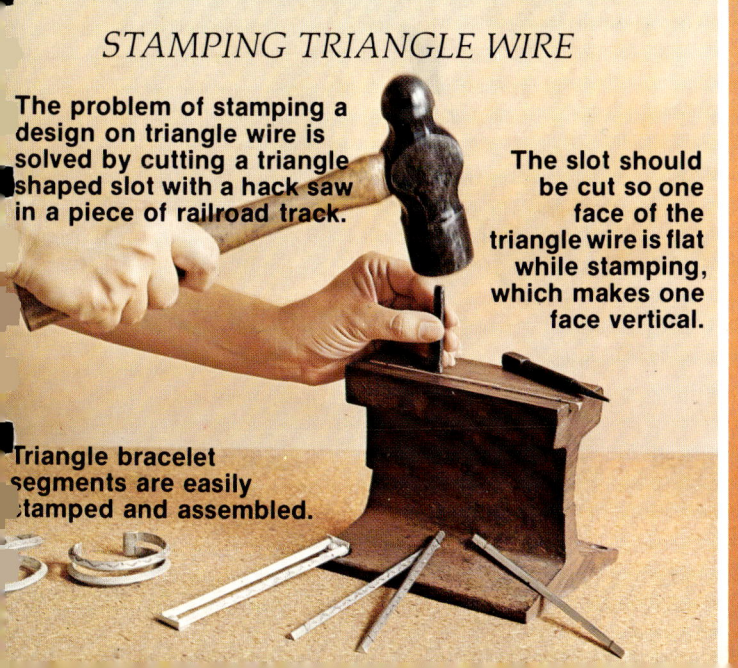

Triangle bracelet segments are easily stamped and assembled.

SETTING OR MOUNTING A STONE

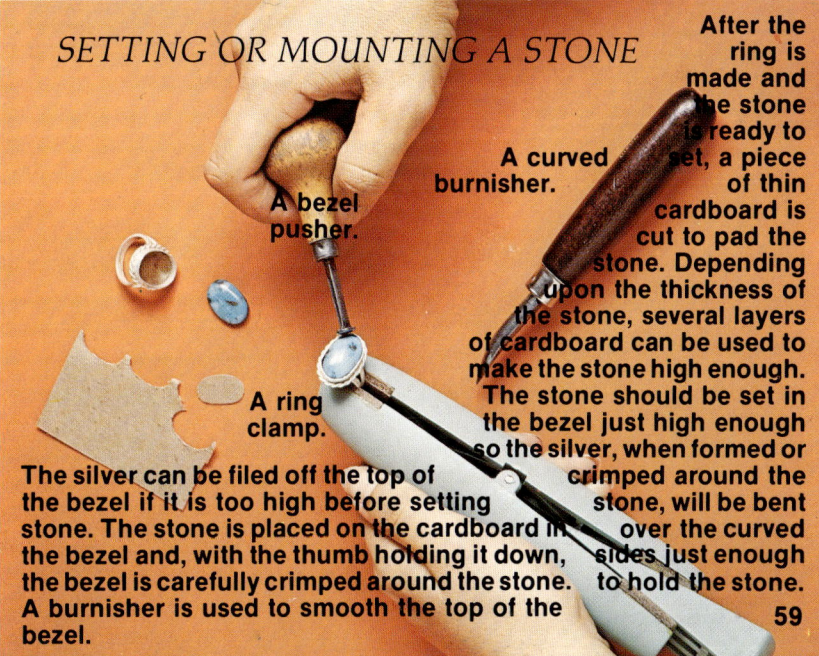

A bezel pusher.

A curved burnisher.

A ring clamp.

After the ring is made and the stone is ready to set, a piece of thin cardboard is cut to pad the stone. Depending upon the thickness of the stone, several layers of cardboard can be used to make the stone high enough. The stone should be set in the bezel just high enough so the silver, when formed or crimped around the stone, will be bent over the curved sides just enough to hold the stone.

The silver can be filed off the top of the bezel if it is too high before setting stone. The stone is placed on the cardboard in the bezel and, with the thumb holding it down, the bezel is carefully crimped around the stone. A burnisher is used to smooth the top of the bezel.

59

PICKLING

When soldering silver, it is necessary to paint a flux on the surfaces to be soldered. The flux melts upon heating, protecting the surface from oxidizing and causes the solder to flow more readily. After soldering it is necessary to clean the melted flux and oxides from the surface of the silver. This is done by placing the object in an acid solution called a pickle.

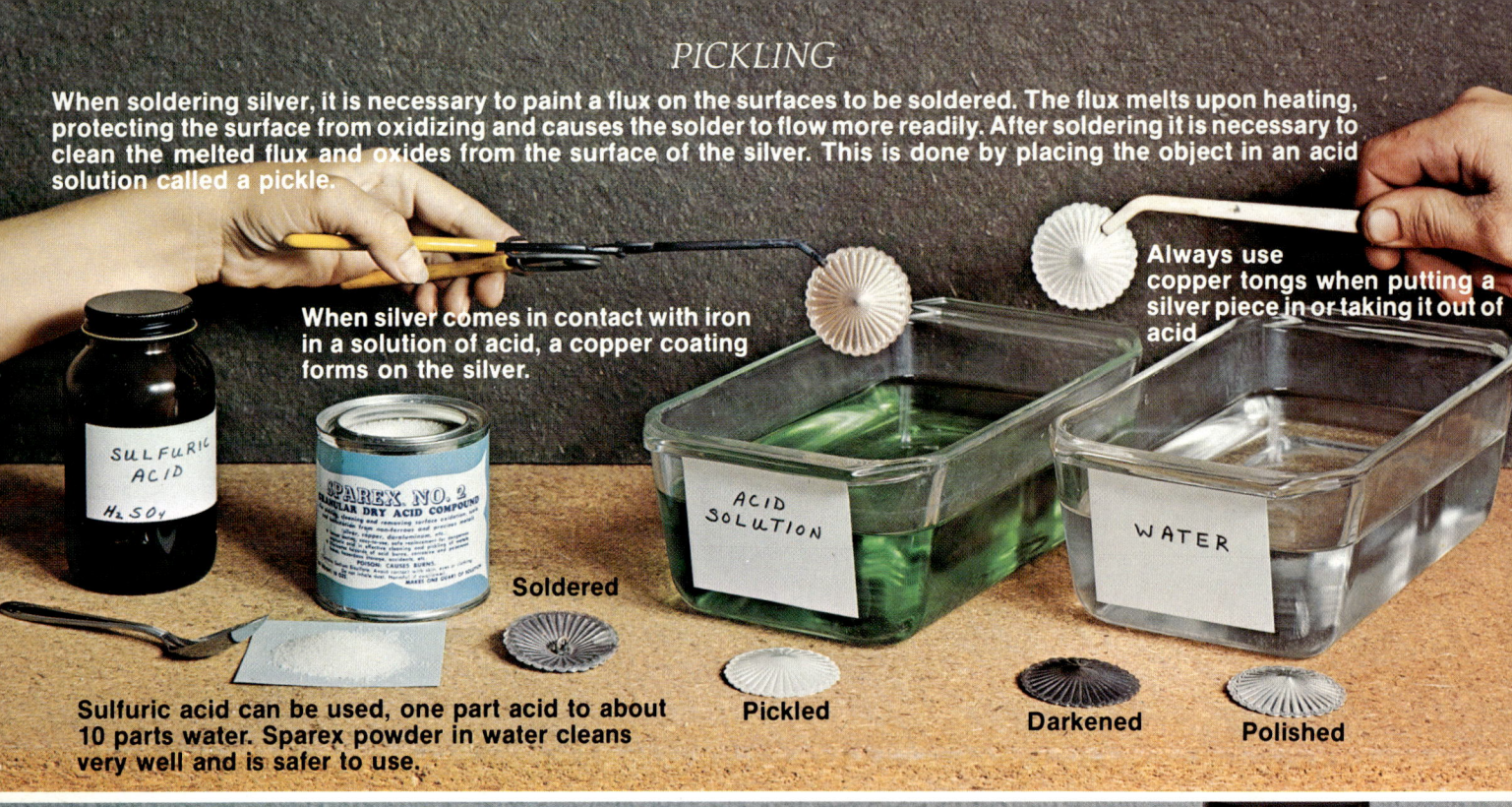

When silver comes in contact with iron in a solution of acid, a copper coating forms on the silver.

Always use copper tongs when putting a silver piece in or taking it out of acid.

Sulfuric acid can be used, one part acid to about 10 parts water. Sparex powder in water cleans very well and is safer to use.

Soldered — **Pickled** — **Darkened** — **Polished**

ANTIQUING OR DARKENING SILVER

The purpose of antiquing or darkening Indian silver jewelry is to create a contrast between the incised design and the polished surface.

Hil-ox is an antiquing or darkening fluid. It works very quickly, keeps well, should be applied with an iron wire.

Sulfurated potash or liver of sulfur, must be mixed with water, darkens rather slowly. Less expensive than Hil-ox but has an objectionable odor of rotten eggs and the solution is good only for a short time.

Cleaned and pickled — **Darkened** — **Polished**

THE WRONG WAY TO HOLD A PIECE OF JEWELRY WHILE BUFFING

Great care must be taken when buffing to hold the piece of jewelry in a position so the wheel will not catch or grab it. If this happens, it can result in serious injury to the worker and damage to the object.

Bobbing compound for fast cutting.

Tripoli for buffing.

Zam for fine polishing. Especially good on turquoise.

Inexpensive safety glasses

THE CORRECT WAY TO HOLD A PIECE OF JEWELRY WHILE BUFFING

Indian jewelry buffing is done on a cloth wheel first with tripoli to smooth the surface and remove scratches and sharp edges, then final polishing with an agent such as zam.

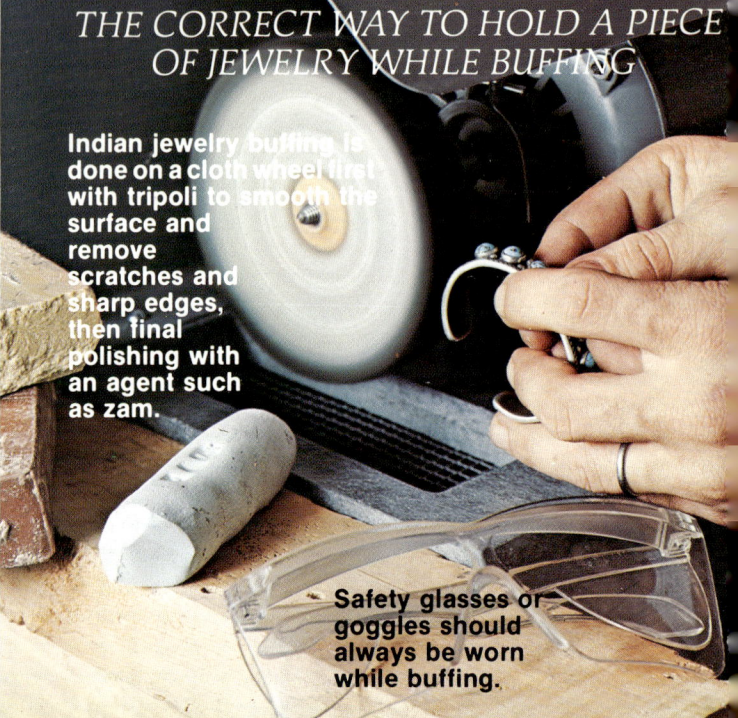

Safety glasses or goggles should always be worn while buffing.

TWISTING SILVER WIRE

The easiest way to twist silver wire is to take a piece of silver wire, fold it in the middle, and clamp the ends criss-cross in a vice. Use a hand drill with a small hook fastened in the chuck, with the loop of wire stretched tight by the hook and the wire is then twisted.

MAKING SILVER BALLS AND DECORATIONS

Silver balls and melted style decorations can easily be made by placing pieces of clean scrap silver with no solder adhering to them on a block of heated charcoal and melting to the shape desired.

They can be cleaned by putting in a pickling solution.

REPAIRING BROKEN STONES.

Cracked stones repaired with strips of silver—sometimes the strips can be decorated or figures of leaves or snakes coiled over the stone.

A stone broken while mounting can be repaired in this manner.

If there are too many cracks or a strip of silver is not advisable, stones can be repaired with epoxy colored to match the matrix with a little dry color, and when hard, filing off the excess and then lightly buffing.

When a stone is broken in a piece of jewelry it can be attractively mended by forcing the bezel away from the stone at both sides of the crack. Then forming a strip of 28 gauge silver across the crack and down into the space made between the bezel and the stone. It will be more permanent if a small amount of epoxy is worked down into the crack and around the bezel before pushing or crimping it back in place.

Sterling Silver specifications

SHEET SILVER

Gauge	$\frac{1}{1000''}$	Wt 1"x6"	Wt. 6"x36"
14	.064	2.10	75.6
16	.051	1.65	60.3
18	.040	1.35	48.6
20	.032	1.00	38.6
22	.025	.85	29.4
24	.020	.65	23.4
26	.016	.50	18.6
28	.013	.40	14.6
30	.010	.35	12.1
32	.008	.25	9.2

Sheet silver comes 6" wide, length to 36".

Wire is sold by type and gauge.

TRIANGLE WIRE

No.	Base	Ht.	Length per oz.	Oz. per foot
1	.380"	.225"	3¾"	3.53
1½	.325	.200	5"	2.45
2	.258	.160	7"	1.65
3	.215	.097	13½"	.83
4	.175	.090	22½"	.66
5	.156	.111	17½"	.68
6	.122	.095	24"	.52
7	.103	.081	30"	.33
8	.080	.064	5'7"	.245

LOW DOME WIRE

No.	Base	Ht.	Length per oz.	Oz. per foot
1	.608"	.077"	4¾"	2.05
2	.515	.065	6¾"	1.70
3	.412	.062	10½"	1.19
4	.232	.072	13½"	1.03
5	.170	.040	31"	.45

ROUND WIRE

Ga.	$\frac{1}{1000''}$	Length per oz.	Oz. per foot
4	.204	5"	2.140
6	.162	9"	1.350
8	.128	15"	.852
10	.102	24"	.536
12	.081	36"	.337
14	.064	5'	.212
16	.051	7'6"	.133
18	.040	12'	.084
20	.032	19'	.053
22	.025	30'	.033
24	.020	48'	.0208

HALF-ROUND WIRE

Ga.	$\frac{1}{1000''}$	Length per oz.	Oz. per foot
2	.257	8"	1.650
4	.204	13"	1.110
6	.162	18"	.680
8	.128	28"	.424
9	.114	32"	.313
10	.102	42"	.250
12	.081	6'	.170
13	.072	7'	.145
14	.064	9'6"	.120
16	.051	15'	.065
18	.040	24'	.042

SQUARE WIRE

Ga.	$\frac{1}{1000''}$	Length per oz.	Oz. per foot
6	.162	7½"	1.750
8	.128	11"	1.085
10	.102	18"	.665
12	.081	28"	.415
14	.064	45"	.265
16	.051	6'	.155
18	.040	9'4"	.105

Weights & lengths given are approximate. Silver is sold by weight, not length.

TUBING, sterling seamless			
	O.D. gauge	WALL gauge	Wt. per Ft. in Oz.
○	7	20	.724
○	9	26	.350
○	10	28	.225
○	12	26	.217
○	14	30	.125

HALF ROUND BEAD WIRE		
Gauge	Thickness	Wt. per Ft. in Oz.
6	.162	.655
7	.144	.408
9	.114	.277
12	.081	.128
14	.064	.101

This handy ring size chart will give an idea of the size of a ring when the ring is laid flat on the paper with the inside diameter of the ring almost covering the printed circle. For better accuracy and to measure the finger size, a metal ring gauge should be used but some of these are only accurate to within 1/4 of a size.

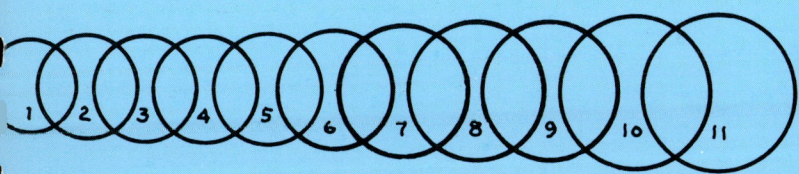

The most accurate tool to measure a ring by is a graduated steel ring mandrel.

ROUND BEAD WIRE		
Gauge	Thickness	Wt. per Ft. in Oz.
4	.204	1.50
6	.162	.95
8	.128	.65
10	.101	.38
12	.081	.24

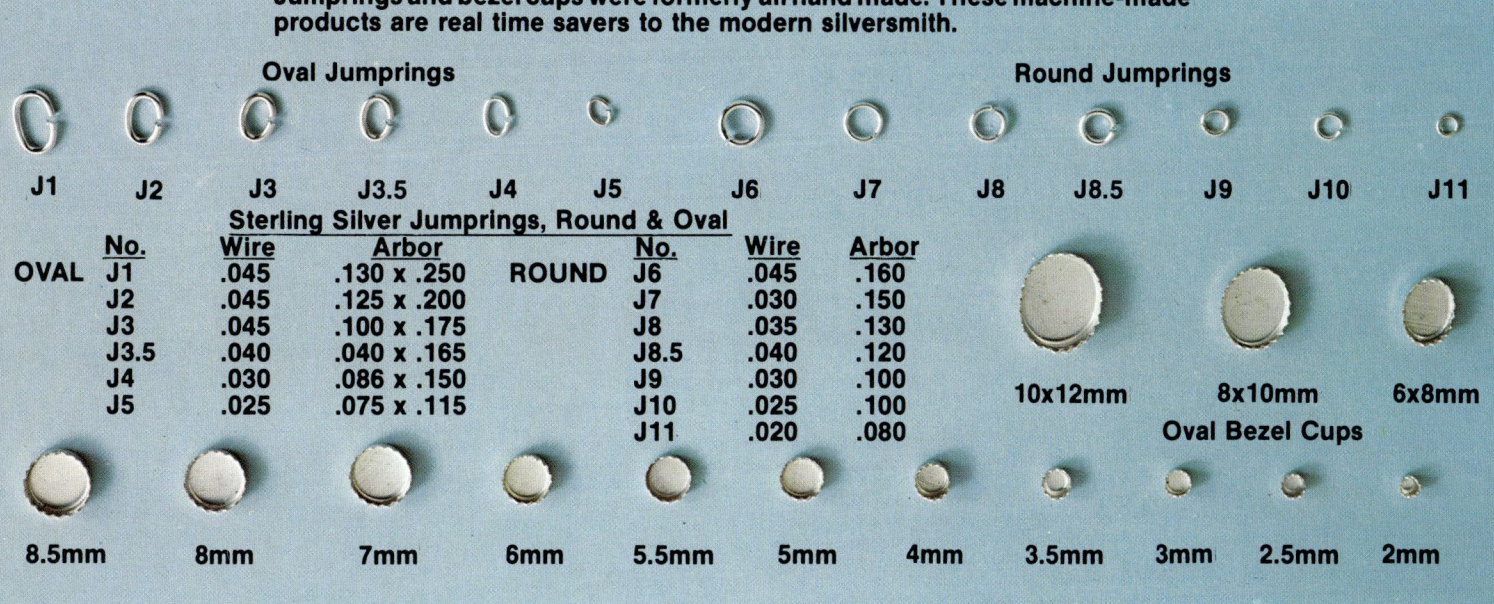

Jumprings and bezel cups were formerly all hand made. These machine-made products are real time savers to the modern silversmith.

Sterling Silver Jumprings, Round & Oval

OVAL	No.	Wire	Arbor	ROUND	No.	Wire	Arbor
	J1	.045	.130 x .250		J6	.045	.160
	J2	.045	.125 x .200		J7	.030	.150
	J3	.045	.100 x .175		J8	.035	.130
	J3.5	.040	.040 x .165		J8.5	.040	.120
	J4	.030	.086 x .150		J9	.030	.100
	J5	.025	.075 x .115		J10	.025	.100
					J11	.020	.080

Oval Bezel Cups: 10x12mm, 8x10mm, 6x8mm

8.5mm, 8mm, 7mm, 6mm, 5.5mm, 5mm, 4mm, 3.5mm, 3mm, 2.5mm, 2mm

This bracelet and ring gauge is available, printed on aluminum, from jewelry supply stores.

BRACELET GAUGE

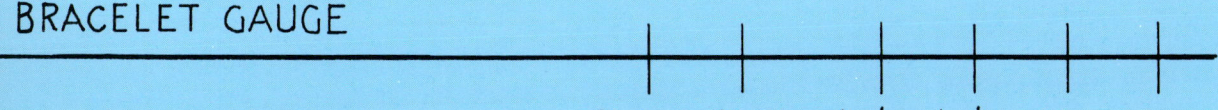

Babies Children Ladies Small Ladies Large Men Small Men Large

RING SHANK GAUGE

0 1 2 3 4 5 6 7 8 9 10 11 12 13 14

A very useful gauge to use for getting an approximate size when making rings and bracelets. When making custom jewelry it is a good idea to get a correct measurement by using a strip of paper wrapped around the wrist or finger. The finger measurement is a complete circle of the finger. The bracelet measurement should be about one inch shorter than the complete circle of the wrist.

Heavier shanks need to be cut longer than lighter ones because of the bending.

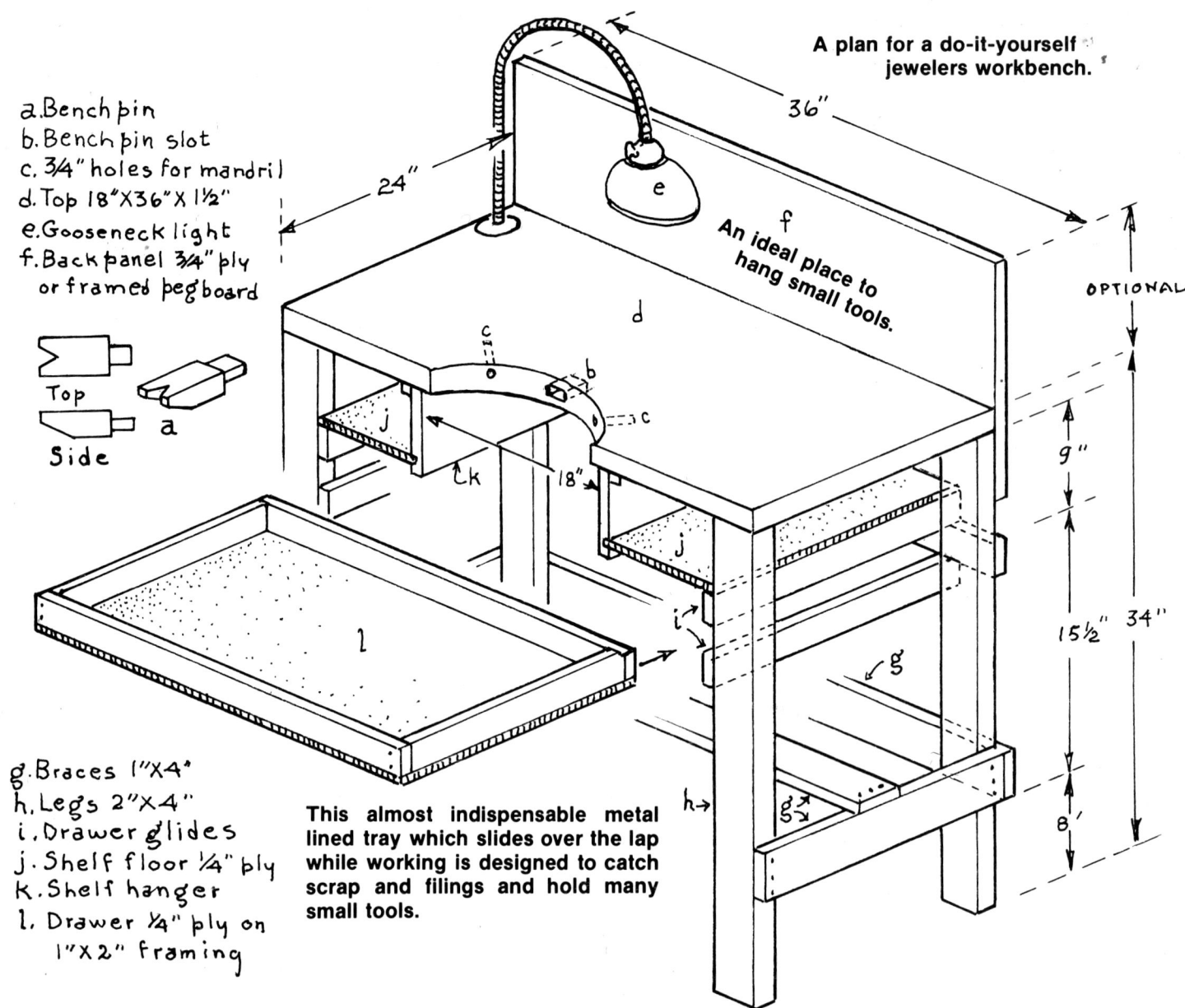

ACKNOWLEDGEMENTS

The greatest debt I owe for much of the information in this book is to the many Indian silversmiths who have shared with me, during the 35 years, their knowledge, their skill and their friendship. To them, and many more, I would like to express my deepest gratitude for making this book possible.

Especially to John Adair who has been a longtime friend and whose wonderful book The Navajo and Pueblo Silversmiths has been a classic down through the years. This book alone has been a great help.

I would also like to show special appreciation to:

Mr. Mark Bahti of Tom Bahti Indian Arts, Tucson, Arizona, for the loan of many pieces of the jewelry.

Mr. Richard Barrett II for his generous assistance, silversmithing skills and advice.

Ethel Branson for her assistance and advice.

Pamela Ray for her assistance in layout and arrangement.

Eveli Sabatie for her encouragement and generous assistance in reading and correcting the manuscripts.

Mr. Jim Tradup who has given me valuable advice from his great store of knowledge in color printing and publication.

To Phil Woodard for his generous loan of tools and equipment.

Thanks is also extended to the following people not mentioned elsewhere in the book:

Connie Ash	Pat Harrison	Nancie Mahan
Dr. W.P. Bemis	John Koffron	Stanley Mahan
Peggy Bahti	Ivan Lytle	Yolanda Moreno
John Cadorini	Danny McGuire	Joe Scheerens
Vic Donahue	Patrick T. Houlihan	Cris Selser
Larry Fuller	Dianne Mahan	Alice Weshe
Vivian Green		

SUPPLIERS OF TOOLS, EQUIPMENT, MACHINERY AND TURQUOISE

Indian Jewelers Supply Co.
601 East Coal Avenue - Box 1774
Gallup, NM 87301
Catalog $5.00

Rio Grande Jewelers Supply
6901 Washington, N.E.
Albuquerque, NM 87109
Order toll free 1-800-545-6566
New Mexico # (505) 345-8511
Free Catalog Available